HOW TO BE A ROMAN

A Day In The Life Of A Roman Family

PAUL CHRYSTAL

First published 2017

Amberley Publishing
The Hill, Stroud
Gloucestershire, GL5 4EP

www.amberley-books.com

British Library Cataloguing in Publication Data.
A catalogue record for this book is available from the British Library.

ISBN 978 1 4456 6564 1 (print)
ISBN 978 1 4456 6565 8 (ebook)

Typeset in 9.5pt on 12.5pt Sabon.
Origination by Amberley Publishing.
Printed in the UK.

CONTENTS

Heracles and Omphale fresco, Pompeii, National Archaeological Museum of Naples, AD 45–79. (Photographer: Stefano Bolognini.)

An early example of a dysfunctional family of sorts: Lydian queen Omphale kept Hercules as a slave. She bought him from Hermes, who offloaded him following an oracle that declared Hercules must be sold into slavery for three years. Hercules had consulted the oracle to find out what he had to do in order to purify himself, after he murdered his friend Iphitus and stole the Delphic tripod. Eventually, Omphale freed Heracles and took him as her husband. It was shameful for Heracles to serve an oriental woman like this, but there are many references to Heracles doing women's work, wearing women's clothes and holding a basket of wool while Omphale got on with her spinning. All of this would have been anathema to our family, as you will see on the following pages…

INTRODUCTION

This is a one day snapshot of day-to-day life in the early empire of ancient Rome, as seen through the eyes of a typical Roman household: husband, wife, son, daughter, and various slaves. It takes you on an exciting journey through the Romans' daily routine from early morning to the middle of the night.

By following this Roman family through their day, this book explains many aspects of a typical Roman's daily routine: work, play, religion, politics, school, military matters, eating, leisure, and bathing.

When you have finished the book, you will come away with a comprehensive picture of what life was like for the typical, relatively well-off family in Rome, and for their slaves. Using a family, as opposed to the usual Roman, is important because it allows us to shed light on the lives of Roman wives and mothers, and on girls – so different from the lives of men and boys; slaves were, of course, different again. Casting a family enables us to give a broader view of the family's different, individual activities and attitudes.

The facts are the facts, so the information in the book is based on and taken from real evidence found in the extensive literature, inscriptions, archaeology, visual arts, and graffiti.

PART ONE

THE ROMAN DAY

We should first look at how the Roman day fits into the other parts of the Roman calendar. Here are the Roman months of the year:

Januarius (January) named after the god Janus: 29 days in the Republican calendar/31 in the Julian

Februarius (February) named after the Februa festivals, which were celebrated at the end of the Roman year: 28 days/28 days

Martius (March) named after the god Mars: 31/31

Aprilis (April) named after the Etruscan god Aprilis: 29/30

Maius (May) named after the goddess Maia: 31/31

Junius (June) named after the goddess Juno: 29/30

Julius (July) named after Julius Caesar, originally named Quintillis, the 5th month: 31/31

Augustus (August) named after Augustus Caesar, originally Sextilis, the 6th month: 29/31

September – the 7th month: 29/30

October – the 8th month: 31/31

November – the 9th month: 29/30

December – the 10th month: 29/31

Total Days: Republican calendar: 355; Julian calendar: 365

Each month was divided into the *Calends*, the first of the month; the *Nones*, the 5th or the 7th; and the *Ides*, the 13th or the 15th – as in 'beware the Ides of March'.

In the late Republic the chaos in the calendar was just about as bad as the political chaos that prevailed in Rome circa 46 BC. The months were out of sync by several months in relation to the seasons. Julius Caesar resolved to do something about this, so he consulted the time experts of the day – the Egyptians. They calculated the length of the actual solar year to be 365.25 days and the winter solstice as 24 December. Julius Caesar's new Julian Calendar followed the solar year, rather than lunar, with a total of 365 days against 355. The old intercalary month was consigned to the dustbin of history and the leap year – adding, as we do today, a day to February every fourth year – was born. In 46 BC the calendar had to be corrected before the new one could begin, so three intercalary months were added at the start of the new year. The year 46 BC, therefore, or 707 AUC to the Romans, lasted for fifteen months and was 445 days long.

Caesar, never missing an opportunity for self-promotion, renamed Quintilis, the fifth month, Julius (July), after himself. Not to be outdone, the first Emperor, Augustus, did likewise to Sextilis, changing it to August, and may have transferred a day from February to August to make his month the same length as Caesar's. All of this had to be endured until 1582 when the Gregorian calendar was introduced by Pope Gregory XIII as a refinement of the Julian calendar, and is recognisable as the western calendar we still use today.

The Romans were extremely superstitious, so it is no surprise to learn that astrology dictated the splitting of the week into seven days to reflect the seven planets thought then to govern the universe:

Dies Saturni	Day of Saturn	Saturday
Dies Solis	Day of the Sun	Sunday
Dies Lunae	Day of the Moon	Monday
Dies Martis	Day of Mars	Tuesday
Dies Mercurii	Day of Mercury	Wednesday
Dies Jovis	Day of Jupiter	Thursday
Dies Veneris	Day of Venus	Friday

The day itself was split into twenty-four hours: twelve hours of daylight and twelve hours of darkness. These hours were of equal length, which caused a problem because the length of an hour, and the hour itself, varied according to the season of the year when the hours of light and darkness changed: shorter hours in winter and longer hours in summer. The Romans called the hours of the day *hora prima* (first hour), *hora secunda* (second hour), and so on. Sunrise was around 4.15 a.m. at the summer solstice, 6.00 a.m. in spring and autumn, and 7.30 a.m. in winter. Sunset fluctuated from approximately 7.30 p.m. at the summer solstice, to 6.00 p.m. in spring and autumn, and to 4.30 p.m. in winter.

Where you were in the empire, and who you were, determined when the day was said to start. Some said the day started at sunrise, the Romans said midnight, while Athenians and Jews went for sunset. The Romans further divided their day into other periods, including midnight, cockcrow, hush of night, and the dying day. Night was divided into four watches – indicative of Rome's militaristic society – because a guard could not keep watch all night; the fourth watch of night was just before dawn.

For our purposes it seems logical and obvious to start the day at dawn, whereas most Romans woke up and proceed through until the dead of night.

PART TWO

A ROMAN FAMILY'S DAY

Meet The Priscuses

Our family is fairly typical of a 'middle class', relatively well-off elite Roman family. The father, Gaius Octavius Lucius Javolenus Priscus, is a lawyer from Umbria who once commanded the Legio IV Flavia Felix, stationed near Burnum, in Dalmatia (Croatia), and who is now working in Rome, having recently served as a jurist in Britannia. He later went on to serve as governor of Germania Superior, then of Syria at the beginning of Trajan's reign (AD 98), was *proconsul* of Africa in 101/2, and finally a *pontifex* (a priest). His wife is Caecilia, a descendent of the ancient Caecilia family. Their son Julius, fifteen, and daughter Octavia, eleven, make up the family, along with six slaves – three men and three women. Two other children died earlier in childbirth; nothing unusual about that.

The Priscus family lives on the Palatine, a leafy part of central Rome on one of the seven hills. From up here you can look down on the Roman Forum on one side, and on the Circus Maximus on the other. In recent years Augustus (27 BC – AD 14), our first emperor, and Tiberius (AD 14 – AD 37) both had their palaces on the Palatine. Augustus – or Octavian as he was known then – was actually born here in the Palatine House.

As we speak, the Flavian Palace is under construction – the emperor Vespasian (AD 69 – AD 79) laid the first stone and Titus, the current emperor (AD 79 – AD 81), continued the work. Twelve or so years later, as it neared completion under Domitian in AD 92, the poet Statius marvelled at its splendour:

> This huge building is truly awesome. It's not famous for a mere one hundred columns, but for as many as could shoulder the gods and the whole of heaven if Atlas took the day off. Jupiter's palace is next door and can only gawp at it; the gods rejoice that you, Marcellus, live in a similar house.[1]

They say that the Lupercal cave is here too – the place where the wolf suckled Romulus and Remus before they went on to found Rome in 753 BC, and the origin of our famous Lupercalia festival.

Martial describes the daily grind that is life in Rome; the type of day the Priscus family may have had to deal with on a frequent basis, aspects of which would have resonated with Javolenus Priscus as a lawyer:

The first and second hours grind down those attending the morning court sitting; the third gets shouty lawyers going; before the fifth hour, Rome offers out her various tasks; the sixth gives peace and quiet to the weary; the seventh brings an end. The eighth and ninth is just right for the oil-shiny wrestler; the ninth commands us to squash down on the heaped up couches for dinner. The tenth hour, Euphemus, is poetry time.

Martial, *Epigrams* 4, 8

Right: Gallia Placida (AD 388–450), on the right, and her family – a typical family portrait, which would have been familiar in AD 80. In the Museo di Santa Giulia, Brescia; she is with the future emperor Valentinian III and Honoria. It forms part of the Croce di re Desiderio (eighth–ninth centuries).

Below: Rome in the late first century AD; the Palatine Hill is just to the west of the Flavian amphitheatre.

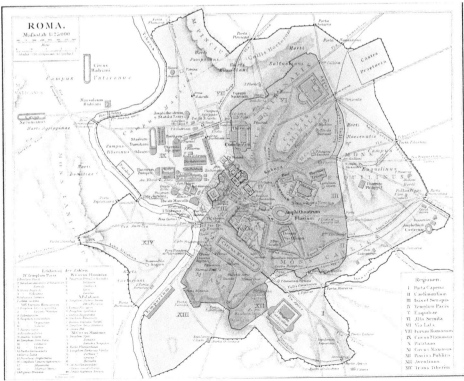

Above left: Sarcophagus of the Dioscures, detail depicting a marriage. Marble, later part of the fourth century. Musée de l'Arles et de la Provence Antiques. It shows a Roman couple joining hands; the bride's belt may show the knot symbolizing that the husband was 'belted and bound' to her; he would untie the knot in their nuptial bed. Photographer Ad Meskens.

Above right: Breastfeeding scene depicting a mother and her husband in close attendance.

AD 80

The year is AD 80, a leap year starting on a Saturday of the Julian calendar. The Priscuses knew it as the Year of the Consulship of Augustus and Domitianus, or year 833 *Ab urbe condita*, from the founding of Rome. There was a lot going on:

- The reigning emperor was Titus or, officially, Titus Flavius Caesar Vespasianus Augustus (30 December AD 39 – 13 September AD 81) who succeeded his father Vespasian – the first Roman emperor to accede to the throne after his own biological father.
- Rome is just settling down after the catastrophic eruption of Mount Vesuvius, which resulted in the overwhelming of Pompeii and Herculaneum and much of their populations – a natural disaster of the first order. Titus provided substantial aid to start rebuilding and to help the displaced and homeless. Pliny the Elder, the scientist, died in the eruption.
- Emperor Titus completes and inaugurates the Flavian Amphitheatre or Colosseum with a generous 100 days of games with free admission and free fast food.
- The construction of Lullingstone villa in Britannia begins. You can see a Romano-Christian chapel there – some of the earliest evidence of Christianity in Britain.
- In Britannia, Gnaeus Julius Agricola reaches the River Tyne–Solway Firth frontier zone. He builds a fleet to help him conquer Caledonia; he circumnavigates the island and proves that Britannia is an island. He launches his invasion of Caledonia.

The emperor Titus.

- Legio II Adiutrix is stationed at Deva Victrix (Chester). This 'Rescuer' Second Legion was founded in AD 70 by Vespasian and was originally composed of Roman navy marines of the *classis Ravennatis*. It was blooded in Germania Inferior during the Batavian rebellion and then followed Quintus Petillius Cerialis to Britannia to deal with the rebellion led by Venutius before helping to subdue Scotland and Wales from its springboard in Deva from AD 78.[2]
- The original Pantheon in Rome is destroyed in a fire, together with many other buildings. This Pantheon was commissioned by Marcus Agrippa during the reign of Augustus (27 BC – 14 AD). It can boast the world's largest unreinforced concrete dome.[3]
- The Eifel Aqueduct – one of the longest aqueducts of the Roman Empire – was completed and carried water 95 kilometres from the hills of the Eifel region to Colonia Claudia Ara Agrippinensium.[4] Most of it was built underground to protect it from weather damage and freezing; the flow of the water was produced entirely by gravity. There are some bridges, one of which is an arched bridge over the Swistbach near Rheinbach, 1,400 metres long and 10 metres high.

Notes

1. Statius (*c.* 45 – *c.* 96 AD); *Silvae* 4, 2, 18ff.
2. Chester.
3. And still is.
4. Present-day Cologne or Köln.

CHAPTER I

COCKCROW: THE NOISY
HOUR BEFORE DAWN

Javolenus Priscus wakes up, or rather is woken up by the usual din at dawn; he does some work and then goes to the barber's.

As with anywhere, the process of getting up in ancient Rome was determined by at least three separate and distinct things. They were: what was on the agenda for the coming day, what time and in what condition one had gone to bed the night before, and noise. The first tends to demand an early morning rise from bed; the second, a somewhat later appearance depending on the events of the previous evening, the time of retiring, and the state in which one retired; the third usually caused a wholly unwanted and untimely awakening.

Fashionable hairstyles on Roman-era Egyptian mummy portraits uncovered at Tebtunis, Egypt. Excavated 1899–1900, the paintings date back to the first and second centuries AD and are believed to have been kept in the home and then added to a mummy upon their subject's death.

The cocks crow. It's still dark, but the slaves are already chattering and clattering about, getting ready for the day ahead. Javolenus could only agree with the epigrammist Martial, who gives us a vivid, if grumpy account of the disturbed Roman's rude awakening in city-centre Rome – indeed, getting a decent night's sleep in the city that never sleeps is quite impossible. In enumerating the manifold, noisy disturbances, Martial provides a sonic picture of those hours before dawn in which a poor man can neither rest nor think in his *cenacula* (apartment), one of many in his *insula* (his tenement block). Outside, coppersmiths, goldsmiths, and money changers rattle and clang their mettle, bakers bawl and noisy revellers laugh their way home, beggars and hawkers add to the din along with teachers already up and teaching:

> Before crested cocks have broken the dawn silence, you bellow out your savage growls and lashes ... dismiss your pupils, prattler, and take as much for keeping quiet as you get for making a din.[1]

Urban living certainly has its drawbacks if it's sleep you want. When the jocular crowd that is last night's noisy revellers wakes Martial, all of Rome seems to be by his bedside, such is the cacophony. Those lucky enough to live in sprawling mansions are insulated from the noise and shuttered from intrusive daylight – they are, in effect, fortunate enough to enjoy country-living in the city – *rus in urbe* – but the only solution for Martial if he wants peace and quiet, and a lie-in, is to repair to his villa out in the real country.

It could be worse, though: sometimes Javolenus Priscus has to put up with anxious and impatient clients banging on his front door even before the crack of dawn.[2]

Even in his mansion, though, there is no guarantee of undisturbed slumber for Javolenus:

> The clattering classes, the slaves, get to work on the cleaning – clanking their buckets, ladders, poles and brooms, armed with sponges, clothes and dusters as they noisily clean, sweep and scrub every nook and cranny, polishing the silver and cleaning the pots.[3]

Javolenus agrees that Juvenal has it just about right when he recently described the frenetic activity that awaited him when a guest was coming to stay:

> There's no peace for your household when a guest's expected. "Sweep the marble floor, rub the columns till they shine, brush down that dead spider up there, and all of its web; you, polish the plain silver, and you, the ornate vases." His master's voice rages, as he stands there holding his cane. You're anxious and miserable, lest your friend should arrive and be offended by the sight of filthy dog mess in the hall, or a portico splashed with mud, though a little slave-boy, with half a bucket of sawdust, can soon put that right.
>
> Juvenal, *Satires* 14, 59–67

As he dozes, Javolenus keeps hearing in his head two famous maxims encapsulating very neatly his, at times reluctant, take on day-to-day life and on living: first Horace's 'seize the day', *carpe diem*, from the early days of the empire, and then much more recently,

Pliny's 'to live is to be awake', *profecto enim vita vigila est.*[4] Belief in the veracity of both impelled many Romans like Javolenus to get up and out of bed and get on with their day: life is short – focus on today. Many, but not all Romans that is. Some were decidedly less industrious and less dynamic; these were the fashionable young men about town whose routines were dictated not by 'business', *negotium*, or 'duty', but by *otium*, the exact opposite. A life of *otium*, as pursued and cultivated first by Catullus and other 'new poets' of the last century, involved being busy doing not very much – apart from chasing women and penning verse, and not very early in the morning at that. Javolenus could not help but secretly envy them their 'bohemian' lifestyle.

With an air of resignation Javolenus Priscus repeated to himself those wise words of the scientist Pliny – 'to live is to be awake' – got up from his bed, reassuring himself that the only people who stayed in bed were, according to the equally wise philosopher Seneca, all-night partygoers and hung-over drunkards.[5] So, like all good Romans, Javolenus Priscus seized the day.

Some Romans, though, make valuable use of those gloomy hours of the day, ensconced in what is called 'lucubration'. This is where a writer or official would busy himself getting some writing done, reading reports or dealing with correspondence. The word comes from the Latin, *lucubratio*, 'night work', which evokes the guttering candlelight by which this work would have been done.

Javolenus Priscus lucubrated most mornings – pressure of work made it inevitable and essential – and he usually felt the better for it, because it left him feeling prepared and ready for whatever the day would bring. Cicero, Horace, and the two Plinys all

Roman hairstyles in the British Museum.

did it – the younger Pliny even visiting the previous emperor Vespasian in the middle of the night on official business. Javolenus Priscus agreed with Pliny when he wrote that working in the lamp-lit darkness gave him a sense of freedom, free from distractions and left to his own thoughts.[6]

Javolenus Priscus' bedroom (*cubiculum*) was purely functional. Cramped, sombrely decorated and shuttered, it was furnished only with a bed (*cubile*) and maybe a wooden chest (*arca*), in which various essential items would be kept, and a chair. Pliny's friends would perch on this chair when visiting while Martial flung his cloak onto his. An earthenware chamber pot (*lasanum*) or urinal (*scaphium*) completed the room. The equally functional bed comprised interwoven strips of webbing or wooden slats, a bolster (*culcita* or *cervical*), and a mattress (*torus*) – the quality of the stuffing (*tomentum*) for which depended on what you could afford: from straw, leaves and reeds, to wool and swan's feathers. Two sheets (*tapetia*) covered the mattress: one to lie on (*stragulum*), the other to pull over (*operimentum*); a quilt, sometimes ornately colourful (*lodix*) went on top and a mat covered the floor (*toral*). The better-off man and wife, like Javolenus and Caecilia, would have had their own individual *cubicula*. Babies had cradles – an example with rockers has been excavated at Herculaneum; sadly the baby's skeleton was still in there, overcome by molten ash.

As was the custom, Javolenus Priscus simply took off his cloak when he went to bed, using it as an extra sheet depending on the weather, and sleeping in his two linen or wool tunics. If he managed to sleep through the early morning hubbub, Javolenus might be

The cock that crowed in a first-century BC mosaic in the Burrell Collection, Glasgow Museums and Art Galleries.

wakened by a slave. As for dressing, the notoriously difficult and annoying toga was worn over the tunics; the dreaded toga was made obligatory by the emperor Claudius at tribunals involving Roman citizens, much to the dismay of all lawyers.[7]

But if the toga was not required then dressing was over in a flash; all that remained was to put on your sandals and you were ready for breakfast – a gulped-down glass of water – and the world outside. There was no need to wash or bathe, that would be taken care of in the afternoon at the public baths or, for the super-rich, in your own private bath room.

Today, though, Javolenus Priscus would first pay a visit to his barber's. The barber shop was a social hub attracting customers from all walks of life, and anyone who just fancied a chat. Meetings were held here, news was swapped, and gossip was gossiped from dawn to the middle of the night. The Roman barbers served as the Internet of the day, with customers 'googling' through enquiring about and expatiating on, everything under the sun to stay informed and up to date. The barber – the *tonsor* – was an important man in most Roman men's lives; he was purveyor of news, sounding board, and confessor all in one.

As he waited his turn, Javolenus Priscus reflected on the fact that in a few years it would be time for Julius, his son, to have that all-important first shave, a rite of passage on his road to manhood.

The actual haircut was a rather perfunctory affair, performed with comb and rudimentary iron or wooden scissors – the fashion of the day was to have your hair trimmed short on the crown; long hair and curls were frowned upon. Martial exposes the ludicrous attempts by Marinus to conceal his age with some injudicious combing-over. To Martial nothing could be uglier.[8] Baldness, though, is generally considered something of a deformity. Indeed, when it comes to hairdressing, little escapes Martial's eagle eye and poisoned pen: he pours unremitting scorn on the fashion for curls, perfume, and face cream – invective that was a literary tradition going as far back as Cicero.[9] Be that as it may, it is probably these fashion-conscious dandies who make some barbers very rich, working from their swish salons. Not for Javolenus Priscus, though, these modern, outré styles.

The emperor was the fashion guru and anyone with political aspirations followed suit; from Tiberius to Trajan, including Titus, clean-shaven was the thing to be. To Martial a man with a beard was no better than a billy goat. Such was the inherent danger of the razor that no one ever shaved themselves; everyone, like Javolenus Priscus, felt much safer in the hands of an expert and professional. Not that it was ever a comfortable experience – the razor was of iron and the only emollient was plain and simple water; the barber's sharpening stone was moistened simply by him spitting on it. Combs were made of wood, ivory, or iron.

As a lawyer Javolenus Priscus was only too aware of the risks involved in having an apparently innocent shave: jurists had been agonising since the time of Augustus to establish guidelines on responsibility and damages when, opting for speed, that blade slipped and delivered bloody scars and wounds; the alternative was to go for a more cautious barber and the interminable torture that involved.[10] Javolenus recalls how Martial has ensured that a particularly savage barber, Antiochus, has gone down in the annals of barber butchery: an appointment with him might lead to an early one-way journey to Hades. Even surgeons deliver less pain when they fix hernias or mend bones;

indeed, after Antiochus has finished with you, you come away with a face like a veteran boxer's, bearing scars that not even a furious wife with her angry talons could have inflicted. Martial concludes that it might be wise to be a billy goat after all, and avoid Antiochus.[11] Post-shave treatment to staunch the bleeding usually came in the form of plasters – made from spiders' webs, olive oil, and stinging vinegar.[12]

Javolenus Priscus knew that there were alternatives available to him: ointments smoothed the chin and hair removers kept a balding head smooth.[13] He could always pay a visit to the depilator who would apply a liniment made from a resin and tar. Indeed, the depilators of ancient Rome had a whole medicine chest of weird and wonderful depilatories made from white vines, ivy gum, donkey fat, she-goat gall bladder, bat's blood or desiccated viper.[14] Simple epilation with tweezers was probably the safest bet.

Javolenus Priscus, however, settled for a regular haircut and a swift shave. This time he declined a manicure and he did not have any corns to cut.[15] Warts were not a problem so he was able to avoid any of the minor surgical procedures the barber routinely carried out. There was work to be done.

Notes

1. Martial 12, 57; 9, 68 1–4, 8–12.
2. Horace, *Satires* 1,1.
3. Juvenal 14, 59–63.
4. Pliny the Elder (AD 23 –AD 79), *Natural History Praefatio* 18.
5. Seneca (4 BC – AD 65), *Letters* 122.
6. Pliny the Younger, *Letters* 3, 5, 8; 9, 36.
7. Claudius (AD 41 - AD 54); see Suetonius, *Claudius* 15.
8. Martial 10, 83; see also 5, 49.
9. Martial 2, 12; 2, 29.
10. Digest 9, 2, 11.
11. Martial 11, 84.
12. Pliny the Elder, *Natural History* 29, 114.
13. Martial 3, 74.
14. Pliny the Elder, *Natural History* 28, 250.
15. Plautus, *Pot of Gold* 267.

CHAPTER II

I AM A ROMAN, A CITIZEN OF ROME

Apart from contemplating the fact that his son would soon take on the responsibilities of manhood, Javolenus Priscus took time to muse on his own 'Roman-ness' and what being a Roman actually meant and involved. This meditation was timely, because he would soon have to explain to Julius the very same things in preparation for his graduation from boyhood to adulthood.

Javolenus was only too aware that it was this idea of 'Roman-ness' that dictated much of what he and his fellow Romans did in their daily life and how they did it. He was also acutely conscious that the empire was a very big place – it had evolved over 800 years and it was made up of people from all over his world. Because of this diversity there was no such thing as a Roman as an identifiable entity or concept. The Roman man and woman is forever changing and evolving, a moving target, in place and in time. The Roman back in fourth century BC Italy was very different from, and quite unrecognisable to, for example, the Romans he had worked with in first century AD Eboracum (York).

But Javolenus Priscus can identify certain qualities that are commonly and consistently attributable to Romans, wherever and whenever they were. Those qualities fall conveniently under the term '*Romanitas*' – a word that was never actually used by the Romans themselves until the third-century AD Roman writer Tertullian.[1] Tertullian's use is pejorative, to describe his fellow Carthaginians who aped Roman ways. Juvenal had said much the same quite recently, vilifying his fellow Romans who were slaves to the ways of Greeks and to all things Greek. To Juvenal, Greece was polluting and diluting *Romanitas*:

> What is more sickening than this: no woman thinks herself beautiful unless she's changed from being a Tuscan to a little Greek bit... Everything has gone Greek: however, it's even more grotesque when Romans have no Latin. They show their fear, their anger, their joys and their worries in Greek; they pour out every secret of their souls in this tongue... You might allow this in a young girl, but will you still be Greeking it when you're pushing eighty-six? Such a way of speaking is surely not right for a little old lady.

> Juvenal 6, 184–191

Martial agreed:

> Laelia, you don't live in Greek Ephesus, or Rhodes, or Mitylene, but in a house in a posh part of Rome; and although your mother was a dusky Etruscan who never wore make-up; and although your father was a hard man from Aricia, you, and I'm ashamed to say it, are a citizen of Roman Hersilia and Egeria – yet you keep bombarding me in Greek.
>
> Martial 10, 68

The concept of *Romanitas* took on an air of respectability and nobility in tune with the 'grandeur that was Rome'. For Javolenus Priscus and his contemporaries it came to mean quintessential 'Roman-ness' – what it means to be a Roman and how the Romans regarded themselves; it defined a true Roman; it encapsulated the Roman ideal.

Despite the best efforts of foreign influences, there was always an element of conservatism and traditionalism running through the marrow of the Roman people. This evolved over time into a national character that had its roots in the early humble, agricultural days and was characterised as demonstrating hard work, honesty, exuding *gravitas* (dignified, serious or solemn conduct), and being diligent in every way; moreover, the true Roman lived by and respected the *mos maiorum* – the way the ancestors had gone about things. He, or she, was expected to be dutiful, to exhibit *pietas*, in every

The Pantheon in 2016, by night.

sphere of life: towards family, friends, country, fellow citizens, comrades in arms, and gods. *Romanitas, gravitas,* and *pietas* did indeed define the Roman.

Javolenus Priscus was clever enough to know that there was always a difficult line to be drawn between diversity and xenophobia (fear and suspicion of foreigners). His history lessons had told him about the arch-conservative Cato the Elder (234–149 BC). As champion of the *mos maiorum* and despiser of things Greek, Cato spoke out sternly against what he saw as a period of moral decline and the erosion of the sturdy principles on which Rome had lain her foundations.[2] Among other things, he identified the growing independence of the women of Rome as an ominous ingredient in this.[3] The defeat of Hannibal at Zama in 202 BC, the victory over the Macedonians at Pydna in 168, and the final extinguishing of the Carthaginian threat in 146 BC all allowed Rome to relax more and encouraged an unprecedented influx of Greek and eastern influences and luxuries into a receptive Rome.[4] In 191 BC Cato defiantly addressed a Greek audience in Athens in Latin.[5]

Cicero, too, was a stickler for *Romanitas.*[6] The Latin language, or rather the ability to speak it, and the practice of Roman law were equally potent badges of Roman-ness; as a lawyer himself, of course, this resonated with Javolenus Priscus:

> Ordinary men, born in obscurity, go to sea and they go to places which they have never seen before; places where they can neither be known to the men among whom they have arrived, nor where they can always find a lawyer. However, due to this singular faith in their Roman citizenship, they think that they will be safe, not only among our own magistrates, who are constrained by fear of the law and of public opinion, but also with our fellow citizens who are joined with them, among many other things, by a common language and laws; but wherever they come they think that this will protect them.
>
> Cicero, *In Verrem* 2, 5, 167

In the *Brutus*, 37, 140, he is even more explicit, declaring that it is a matter of shame not to know Latin; a facility for Latin was a mark of the good Roman citizen. Nearer Javolenus Priscus' own time, Suetonius tells us that the emperor Tiberius believed it important that soldiers in the Roman army be able to speak Latin from an incident when he refused a Greek soldier permission to reply in Greek when summonsed to give evidence.[7] The conquering Roman army was the prime vehicle for and deliverer of 'Romanisation' when it consolidated the lands into the Roman Empire: speaking Latin was a key element in that 'Romanisation'. There is good evidence that foreign troops and mercenaries in the Roman army learned Latin.

As a lawyer, Javolenus Priscus knew that wills had to be written in Latin; that tombstones for Roman soldiers, be they Roman or foreign, throughout the empire are always in Latin, except for Roman Egypt where Greek is used. To the Romans, Latin was the only language of any significance; it would not have occurred to them to learn a 'barbarian' tongue – Latin symbolized civilisation. In about AD 30 the historian Valerius Maximus reported how Roman magistrates throughout the Roman world used Latin as a weapon in upholding Roman *maiestas* (greatness) when they insisted that court proceedings be in Latin and that the Greeks use interpreters to translate into Latin.[8] Speaking Latin inculcated respect for Roman power and symbolised Roman-ness. Latin was an enduring emblem of *Romanitas.*

This fairly typical funerary relief shows Lucius Vibius, his freedwoman wife Vecilia Hila, and their son Lucius Vibius Felicius Felix – his last name a pun on his *cognomen*. They all attempt to display 'Romanness' (*Romanitas*), with father styled like Julius Caesar, mother with a Livia-type hairstyle, and son like an Augustan boy. It is from the end of the first century BC; originally published in *Greek and Roman Portraits*, A. Hekler (New York, 1902). Now in the Vatican Museum.

Javolenus Priscus resolved to get on with his day, secure in the knowledge that he would use his own personal *Romanitas* to good effect in the courts and that, in turn, he would be protected by the *Romanitas* shown by others.

Notes

1. Tertullian (*c.* 155 – *c.* 240 AD), an early North African Christian, who coined it in his De Pallio, *On the Cloak* (4, 1).
2. Plutarch, Cato 23, 1–3; Polybius 31, 24.
3. Livy 24, 2–4; Aulus Gellius 7, 6–8.
4. Various suggestions for the start and or cause of the decline have been made: Polybius, 31, 25 ascribes it to the victory over Macedonia; L. Calpurnius Piso (Pliny *Natural History* 17, 38, 244) goes with 154 BC; Appian, *Bellum Civili* 1, 7 for the end of the war in Italy; Livy 39, 6, 7 prefers 186 BC; Valleius Paterculus, *Historiae Romanae*, and Sallust, *Catilina* 10 opt for the end of the Third Punic War.
5. Plutarch, Cato 12, 4–5.
6. Cicero (106 BC-43 BC), philosopher, politician, lawyer, orator, and consul.
7. Tiberius was emperor from AD 14 to AD 37. Suetonius, *Tiberius* 71.
8. Valerius Maximus (*c.* 20 BC – *c.* AD 50), 2, 2, 2.

CHAPTER III

THE LADY OF
THE HOUSE RISES

Meanwhile, in another room, Caecilia, the lady of the house – the *matrona* – had got out of bed and was preparing for her day.

Generally speaking shared beds were the preserve of the less well-off, but Caecilia's roomy villa now allowed her the luxury of a separate room.

Caecilia prided herself on being a good Roman *matrona* – a good wife to Javolenus Priscus, a good mother to his children, and once a good daughter to her late father. Funerary inscriptions provide the prescription for a *matrona*; they idealise and lionise what was expected of the Roman wife and mother and, in some instances, reveal real love between wives and their husbands, between husbands and their wives. Until marriage, a girl or woman was under the power of her father and, after marriage, was expected to take an active but discreet role in the running of the marital home, under the power of her husband.

As a *matrona* she should be virtuous, strong-willed (but not obtrusively so), conversational, modestly dressed, loyal, compliant; she must look after her children, particularly their education. This one-man-woman – *univira* – would be preoccupied with wool-working and looking after the home; both powerful badges of the good wife. As time went by, richer women acquired a greater degree of domestic authority and influence, delegating mundane and menial tasks to slaves and enjoying a social life outside the home. They nevertheless remained under the control of fathers, husbands, and guardians, although increasing wealth and independence allowed them to take more of the initiative in public and in family matters – but they were never able to shrug off the traditional suspicion and discrimination often vocalised by Roman men when they did overstep their duties as *matronae*. Tombstone inscriptions apart, there is evidence of mutual love and affection; Martial gives us a touching picture of the fifteen-year-long marriage between Calenus and Sulpicia where devotion to each other was obviously paramount.[1]

Even in Caecilia's day Livia, Augustus' wife of fifty-two years standing, was still the woman to emulate, some fifty-one years after her death. Livia from the start acted in consort with her husband, advising him on policy decisions while running her own personal affairs. At the same time, though, she was very much the role-model *matrona*, dressing modestly in the *stola*, working the wool, wearing little jewellery, her hair conservatively done, often in *nodus* style with its old Republican overtones as championed by Octavia, her sister-in-law; she attended to the relatively modest household nearby on the Palatine, striving for a child, an heir for her husband.

Above left: Fresco showing a woman looking in a mirror as she dresses or undresses her hair. From the Villa of Arianna at Stabiae (*Castellammare di Stabia*), Naples National Archaeological Museum.

Above right: Portrait of a Roman woman (Vibia Matidia? b. AD 80) Roman, in the Musei Capitolini. View from behind showing the elaborate hairstyle in fashion at the time.

Matronae were recognisable in the street by the *palla*, a woollen rectangular shawl draped over a *stola* (or *insita*, the shoulder straps of the *stola*). This *stola* was a long, ankle-length dress; hair was kept under control with *vittae* (hair bands that were sometimes studded with jewels). *Matronae* covered their hair in public so the *palla* doubled as a hooded cloak or veil. Such clothes instantly marked out the *matrona* from unmarried girls, women without Roman citizenship, adulteresses, prostitutes, and other women of dubious occupation such as dancers, actresses, and anyone else working in the entertainment or catering industries. The words *stola*, *insita,* and *vittae* themselves became metonyms for respectability and chastity: Ovid uses them when he disingenuously dissuades *matronae* from reading his *Ars Amatoria*; Martial mentions the decency (*pudor*) of the *stola* – Valerius Maximus *verecundia stolae,* the modesty of the stola.[2]

The female slaves would have fussed around to help Caecilia with her toilette and dressing, to which extreme care was given at a decidedly leisurely pace. Like her husband, Caecilia would have slept in her underclothes – loincloth, tunic, and *strophium* (a kind of bra, or corset). Despite laws designed to curb extravagance in clothing (particularly elite women's clothing), women loved to dress up in exotic fabrics such as silk damasks, translucent gauzes, and gold cloth, coloured with expensive dyes such as saffron or

Above left: Front view.

Above right: Salonia Matidia (AD 68 – AD 119) was the daughter and only child of Ulpia Marciana and Gaius Salonius Matidius Patruinus. Her maternal uncle was the Roman emperor Trajan to whom she was like a daughter. She was also mother-in-law of Emperor Hadrian. The hairstyle would have been popular around AD 80. From the Via Giolitti, 1874. Now in the Capitoline Museum, Rome.

Tyrian purple. Flashy jewellery, especially brooches, added to the effect; clean, bright clothing radiated respectability and status in women.

Caecilia was no exception, and she paid great attention to and spent much time on her appearance every day. First was the day's make-up and hairstyle. So important was making-up that the Romans had a word for it, *cultus*, which embraced make-up, perfume, and jewelry. Well-off women had a special woman-only room for applying it, and the rich, like Caecilia, had special slaves trained in cosmetics – the all-important *cosmetae*.

Some Roman men were still suspicious of the motives of made-up women; it incited a man's innate insecurity and made him question who his woman was making herself up for. For some, cosmetics were indicative of immorality and were associated with Greeks, orientals, prostitutes, witches, actresses, and dancers. To the misogynist Juvenal 'a woman buys scents and lotions with one thing in mind, adultery.' Nevertheless, many respectable women shrugged off these usually unfounded concerns and slapped on the make-up regardless; Caecilia argued that since the word cosmetics comes from the Greek *kosmetikos*,

Scenes of everyday life from the fourth-century AD estate of Julius found in a house in Carthage. This shows the *domina* selecting jewellery to wear from a box held by a slave; the next shows a woman exhibiting her credentials as a *matrona* with one of the articles of faith: she is telling the world that *lanam fecit* – she works the wool. The third is from baths at Sidi Ghrib near Tunis: here the *domina* is being offered a mirror by one of her slave girls as she completes her toilette. By kind permission of Inga Mantle, who took the photographs, and Caroline Vout, who published them in *Omnibus*, 65 (2013). Now in the National Museum of the Bardo, Tunis.

Above left: Styles in women's hairdressing changed over the years. This page, originally published in *Roman History, Literature and Antiquities* by A. Petrie (London, 1926), depicts changing styles from the beginning of the empire to the early third century AD. The fashionable, extravagant style top right is similar to the Fonseca bust in the Capitoline Museum, Rome. The crown was built up with fillets of wool and was worn on the back or the front. The hair was combed into two parts; the front was combed forwards and built up with curls, while the back was plaited and made into a bun.

Above right: Lady with a curly toupee. Behind the curls the hair is braided in plaits, which originally had been gathered in a nest at the back of the head. Julia, daughter of the emperor Titus, made this fashionable.

meaning a sense of harmony, order, and tranquillity, the use of cosmetics announced that all was well with the world. Not so many years ago, she adds, Ovid characteristically pushed back the boundaries when he wrote one of the world's first make-up manuals.[3]

Had they had the science, then men may have been more concerned about the dangers associated with the industrial usage of some of these cosmetics and the toxic constituents of many of the cosmetics. As it was, women like Caecilia went on applying them, unaware of or unconcerned by the risks – such is the power of vanity. And make-up was not just applied once, in the morning: the warm, hot climate in many parts of the empire, Caecilia's Rome included, required a woman to cleanse and reapply her make-up frequently during the day, if dignity and appearances were to be kept up.

The night before Caecilia cleansed her face using sweat from sheep's wool, which had the additional effect of emitting a stench abhorred by men. Other exotic ingredients for

Above left: An elegant Roman woman in one of the necropoles in Pompeii showing her *stola* and *palla*.

Above right: A *matrona* at her toilette in the Rheinisches Landesmuseum, Trier. Relief from a third-century AD funerary monument depicting four slaves; one does the *matrona's* hair, one holds a perfume flask, the third shows a mirror, while the fourth carries a water pitcher.

cleansers may include fruit juice, seeds, horns, excrement from various animals, honey, herbs, placenta, marrow, vinegar, bile, animal urine, sulphur, vinegar, eggs, myrrh, incense, frankincense, ground-up oyster shells, onions with poultry fat, white lead, and barley with vetch. Caecilia kept a store of many of these ingredients. Bathing in donkey milk worked like a chemical peel but was expensive and out of even Caecilia's expensive reach.

Caecilia craved fair skin, considered by men and women alike to be one of the most important features of Roman beauty. She and her *cosmetae* spent many hours and even more money lightening her dusky skin with various oils and whitening make-up to achieve the desired effect. After a quick bath, perhaps, on would go the face-whitener: this might be chalk powder, white marl, crocodile dung or, ideally, white lead (or *cerussa*), which they called *focus* – a life-shortening habit – or a blend of one or two. Beeswax, olive oil, rosewater, saffron, animal fat, tin oxide, starch, rocket (arugula), cucumber, anise, mushrooms, honey, rose leaves, poppies, myrrh, frankincense, almond oil, rosewater, lily root, water parsnip, and eggs all featured in Caecilia's make-up box at one time or another as whiteners.

Caecilia abhorred any blemishes on her skin: wrinkles, freckles, sunspots, flaky skin were all anathema and she and her *cosmetae* worked ceaselessly to remove, or at least camouflage, them. She found swans' fat, asses' milk, gum Arabic and bean-meal effective with wrinkles and applied the ashes of snails in the fight against cold sores and freckles. In desperation, almost, she often pasted soft leather patches of alum on blemishes to masquerade them as beauty spots – which is exactly what criminals and freedmen use to hide brand marks. If it wasn't on her head, Caecilia's body hair was to be eliminated at all costs, and shaving, plucking, stripping using a resin paste or scraping with a pumice stone were all deployed in this never-ending, and painful, battle.

Despite the quest for a pallid complexion, a little rouge on the cheeks never went amiss, indicative as it was of robust health and fitness. Rouge was made from Tyrian vermillion, rose and poppy petals, *fucus*, red chalk, red root alkanet, and crocodile dung. Red ochre imported from Belgium was high-end and ground into powder. Poisonous cinnabar and toxic red lead were used with little or no concern; bargain-basement alternatives included mulberry juice and leftover wine.

Caecilia paid a lot of attention to her eyes. The ideal eyes were big with long eyelashes. Kohl was the ingredient of choice in eye make-up, made from ashes or soot and antimony, with a pinch of saffron added to improve the smell. It was applied with a rounded stick made of ivory, glass, bone, or wood, dipped first into oil or water, before the application of the kohl. Charred rose petals and date stones might also be used to darken the eyes. Green eyeshadow came from poisonous malachite, blue came from azurite – a deep-blue copper mineral. Dark eyebrows – virtual unibrows – were all the rage and Caecilia used antimony or soot for the desired look.

White teeth were as coveted as white faces, so dentures were popular among some of Caecilia's friends – they were made from bone, ivory, and paste. Perfume was vital, not only because a fragrant woman was thought to indicate a healthy women, but strong scents masked the smell of some of the cosmetics and body odour. Less positively, some Roman men believed that perfumes masked the smell of illicit alcohol consumption. Nevertheless, it was applied liberally, not just to produce a pleasant fragrance but to fend off various illnesses, fevers, and indigestion. Deodorants were concocted from alum, iris, and the use of rose petals was common. Caecilia's slaves added perfume to the family's food and used it as an air freshener.

Next, the *stola*, *instita*, and the *palla* and *zona* were carefully put on.

Hairstyles were everything to Caecilia. How she wore her hair reflected her personality and individuality – hairstyles in women generally were indicative of age, social status, wealth, attractiveness, and sexuality. As with making-up, women like Caecilia spent a lot of time having their hair done and gazing into mirrors; the more complicated the style then the more a woman's hair spoke money: lengthy and intricate hairdos told the world that a woman had time and money in abundance, that she was cultivated. The plain styles adopted by barbarian women and poor Romans simply highlighted their lack of sophistication, civilisation, and wealth, and so it was that Caecilia spent what seemed like an eternity every morning over how to have her hair styled. The woman who helped her, the *ornatrix*, was as important to her as her husband's *tonsor* was to him.

Naturally, she went for the 'tall' styles that were particularly fashionable at the current time. Juvenal ridiculed their height when he compared them to multistorey buildings with 'tiers and storeys piled one upon another on her head'.[4]

Above: Gold armband fashioned as a snake, a gold bracelet, and part of a necklace of gold ivy leaves. All in the Naples Archaeological Museum.

Right: Wall painting portrait of a Roman woman in the Naples Archaeological Museum.

A hairpiece from a Roman woman found in a sarcophagus, which contained a lead coffin and gypsum; presumably the hair was preserved because it was treated before burial. Two cantharus-headed hairpins are still in position. Courtesy of York Museums Trust YORYM 1998.695 [ID 1131]

If she felt like it, Caecilia might choose to wear one of the many wigs she owned. Apart from speed and convenience, wigs provided a quick fix to achieve those 'tall' styles and were versatile. Her wigs were made from human hair – blonde from Germany and black from India; they were particularly prestigious if the hair came from the head of a woman from a conquered civilisation. Wigs had the added advantage of obviating the bother of having to grow one's own hair long; the length needed to create those lofty hairstyles daily probably extended down to the waist.

It says something about the importance of sporting modish hairstyles when Caecilia reveals that even her household busts and statues wear wigs – far cheaper to change the wig when a fashion changes than commission a new piece of statuary.

As for hair dyes, gold dust or a blend of goat's fat and beech ash was used to produce blonde hair or to highlight hair that was already blonde. There was no shortage of hair dying, although the products used sometimes burnt the scalp. Caecilia's dyes came in the form of powders, gels, and bleach. Henna or animal fat was rubbed in as a kind of conditioner. Romans wore a paste at night made from herbs and earthworms to minimise greying while pigeon dung was used to lighten hair. To dye hair black, Pliny the Elder recommends applying leeches that have rotted in red wine for forty days.[5] Achieving red required a concoction of animal fat and beech wood ashes; saffron was needed for gold hair.

Hair loss required the application of a sow's gall bladder, mixed with bull's urine; alternatively, the ashes of a donkey's genitals or the ashes of a deer's antlers mixed with wine would do just as well, depending on what was available at the time. The eternal problem of head lice needed liberal amounts of goat's milk or goat's dung.[6]

As well as the myriad potions and concoctions at her disposal, Caecilia made good and frequent use of curling tongs heated in fire, hairpins, and hairnets. Her pins were made of gold, ivory, crystal, silver or painted bone, often carved with images of the gods.

Make-up fixed, Caecilia deliberated over what jewels to wear. A multitude of earrings, necklaces, diadems, brooches, rings, anklets, and chokers always made this a difficult choice.

Caecilia was now ready to face the world: to compete in beauty and finery with her friends and other women she may encounter, to turn the heads of the men of Rome, take in a little shopping, to play with and educate her children, to organise the slaves and balance the household budget.

Notes

1. Martial 10, 38.
2. Ovid, (43 BC – AD 17) *Ars Amatoria* 1, 31–32; Martial 1, 35, 8–9; Valerius Maximus 8, 3.
3. *Medicamina Faciei Femineae* (Women's Facial Cosmetics).
4. Juvenal 6, 58–9.
5. Pliny the Elder, *Natural History* 32, 23.
6. Pliny the Elder, *Natural History* 28, 51; 28, 46.

Blue perfume flask with a white trail (AD 1–100) and two-part eye make-up container (AD 200–400). (Getty Villa Collection by Dave and Margie Hill / Kleerup from Centennial, CO, USA.)

Chapter IV
The Morning Salutation

Another enduring facet of Roman society was the client-patron system, which prevailed from the earliest days of Rome and was endured by most men of any ambition and who had embarked on the *cursus honorum* – the path of public and military offices.

It was a paternalistic relationship between aristocratic patricians like Javolenus Priscus and lower order plebeians, in which the former helped out the latter with protection and a range of welfare and public service issues.

Essentially, it was an extension of the family, in which the father (*pater*) expected similar demonstrations of *pietas* from his wife and children. Clients would form part of the patron's retinue: the bigger the retinue, the more powerful a patron appeared to be. Success in the senate or at the bar enabled the patron to help more clients and expand his retinue. In elections, the client cast his vote for the patron. In return, the patron looked after the client and his family, gave legal advice and represented him in court (something Javolenus Priscus was well placed to do), and helped the clients financially and in other ways. Over 100 years ago Cicero had explained how the system works:

> Men of the lower orders have one chance only by which to earn favours from men of our rank, or to pay us back for the favours we have given them: namely, attending us as a client and working hard on our political campaigns. For it is neither possible, nor something we or the equites (knights) should request, that they attend their patron for whole days at a time. If they all meet up at our house, if we are sometimes led to the forum, if we are privileged by their attending us for the distance of one basilica, then it looks like we have been respected and honoured diligently. Our lesser friends [in the lower orders] are not busy and they [have the time to] provide this constant attendance; all good and generous men are attended by these lesser men.
>
> Cicero, *Pro Murena* 34

With the empire came the end of popular elections and with it a reduction in the usefulness of client to patron. Clients soon came to be regarded as sycophantic, servile almost and often were no more than hangers-on, looking for a hand-out or, increasingly less often, an invitation to dinner. Seneca and Martial[1] highlight this fawning behaviour and the systematic greed, much of which was evident at the morning reception, the *salutatio*:

> Your clients? None of them attend you for what you are, but for what they can get out of you ... now they're just on look-out for loot; if a lonely old man changes his will, the morning-caller just knocks on another door.
>
> Seneca, *Letters* 19, 4

The only consolation for Javolenus Priscus was that this bankrupt old ritual was even more tiresome for his clients than it was for him. Indeed, some had been waiting for him since before dawn. As it was, he would return to his house, take his place in the *atrium* and receive the clients. Favours would be requested, political support lined up for votes, and he would select those who were to accompany him to his chambers.

The *atrium* was a large room flanked by small guest bedrooms and *alae* (wings). In the middle was an *impluvium*, a marble rainwater basin open to the sky. At the back was the *tablinum*; this is where Javolenus Priscus received his clients.

The days of an invitation to dinner for clients were more or less long gone; now the more convenient practice of handing out a basket of food (*sportula*) for those who qualified to receive such a hand-out was a much simpler and tolerable reward for the clients' attendance. There was even a growing tendency to replace these food handouts with money – a most unpopular move as the amounts given were usually paltry.[2] For

First-century BC bust of Cicero in the
Capitoline Museum.

some unfortunates, though, this was the only source of income. Javolenus Priscus knew all about benefit cheats, where the more unscrupulous among his clients would collect his money and shamelessly move on to the next patron to receive another *sportula* there.

Attendance at the *salutatio* was strictly regulated. Clients were expected to wear a smart toga and were presented to the patron in a pecking order depending on their social status – so, for example, the praetor was seen before the tribune, the freedman before the slave. Clients also had to be careful to address the patron formally as *dominus* (master); Martial tells how a failure to observe this courtesy can have serious financial consequences.[3]

Women were spared all of this, most of the time. A further example of the system being abused and exploited – a kind of benefit fraud – involved those men who thought nothing of carting their supposedly sick or pregnant wives around the *salutationes* with them to elicit sympathy and extra money, or even claiming support for wives who simply did not exist, brazenly indicating instead a curtained but empty litter. Unscrupulous widows too did the rounds in an attempt to evoke sympathy and money for deceased husbands who were former clients.[4]

One good thing Javolenus Priscus recognised in the system was that it functioned as a kind of social support network to help the genuinely poor, even though it was being eroded by the increasing exploitation. His clients banded together to protect each other from thieves and robbers. If one was struck down by misfortune and poverty, the other clients – and he as patron – would club together to provide support offering loans, seeing that a daughter had a dowry, organising a decent funeral and so on.

Javolenus Priscus selects his retinue for the day, a slave checks his list and hands out the *sportula*, and they set of for the courts through the bustling streets of Rome.

Notes
1. Martial 6, 88.
2. Martial 3, 7, Juvenal 1, 95.
3. Martial 6, 88.
4. Juvenal 1, 120–6.

Chapter V

Rome At Work And City Living

As Javolenus Priscus' retinue weaves its way through the buzzing and bustling streets of Rome it passes a myriad of shops, workshops, workers and artisans; men and women and slaves alike, all busy keeping the city, this heart of empire, going.

Every imaginable product, produce, and service was available, with much made on the premises and served from a counter facing on to the street; when the shop closed the shutters came down. Javolenus Priscus passed bakers, florists, ointment sellers, barbers, fruit and vegetable sellers, perfume sellers, blacksmiths, fullers, drug stores, booksellers, copyists, furniture sellers, potters, bronze chasers, goldsmiths, cobblers, butchers, hairdressers, silversmiths, carpenters, honey sellers, stone-cutters, jewellers, wine shops, lamp makers, musical instrument dealers, locksmiths, cutlers, and dress makers. All were vying with each other for trade, shouting out their wares and prices; delivery carts and their mules, handcarts and horses clogged the narrow streets making it virtually impossible for anyone in a litter, like Javolenus Priscus, to make much progress.

Specialisation was the name of the game. We hear of lupin sellers, melon sellers, perfumers and druggists, vendors of mirrors, ivory sellers with tusks on display, goldsmiths with their rings and sellers of pearls, shoe and boot-makers, greengrocers who were market gardeners, fishmongers who were fishermen, and wine sellers who grew vines. The tomb of Eurysaches depicts millers and bakers; there were confectioners and pastry cooks, robe-makers and cloak-makers. Indeed, given the cultural importance of sewing and wool-working it is not surprising to see the plethora of support businesses, which included washermen and washerwomen, fullers, dyers, workers in silk, and embroiderers.

The busiest shops, though, were the olive oil sellers. Everyone needed oil for a whole range of purposes. Oil was used for cooking, for cosmetics, as fuel for lamps, when bathing as a cleansing soap, and in sports such as wrestling. Vast quantities of oil were sold every day in the turbulent streets of Rome.

There were banks too – *tabernae argentariae* – handling currency exchange, taking deposits and making payments. They traded investments and issued letters of credit. Money lending was rife through money lenders – not considered a respectable occupation.

Tanners, furriers, rope-makers, ships' caulkers, ship builders and repairers, carpenters, metal workers all added to the urban mix. Legions of public service workers were there too to increase the congestion and cacophony: demolition workers, masons, muleteers, carters, drovers, boatmen and oarsmen, labourers, stevedores, and porters. Soldiers, sailors, and mercenaries on leave clogged up the streets. Prostitutes outside brothels and cook shops and underneath the arches got in the way. Roadworks, building works, and waterworks all made any journey through the city nothing short of a losing battle.

From the relative comfort of his litter, Javolenus Priscus reflected on the fact that some of his fellow aristocratic professionals looked down on the working and commercial classes. He recalled how Cicero, from his privileged position, describes the most suitable occupations for a gentleman and sneers at the labours of the working classes; nowhere is snobbery and the divisive Roman class system more clearly portrayed:

> As regards trades and other ways of making a living, which ones are to be thought fit for a gentleman and which ones are vulgar? First, those livelihoods which make people like us angry are undesirable, for example, tax collectors and usurers. Also vulgar and ill-suited to a gentleman are all hired workmen whom we pay for manual labour...Those also who buy goods from wholesale merchants to sell on are vulgar because they would get no profits without a lot of bare-faced lying... All mechanics are engaged in vulgar trades: no workshop can have anything liberal about it. Least respectable of all are those trades which cater for sensual pleasures: Fishmongers, butchers, cooks, and poulterers, and fishermen... Add to these perfumers, dancers, and anyone on the stage.
>
> On the other hand, the professions in which either a higher degree of intelligence is required or from which society benefits – medicine and architecture, for example, and teaching – these are fine. Small scale trade is to be considered vulgar... But of all the occupations... none is better than agriculture, none more profitable, none more delightful, none more becoming to a free man.
>
> Cicero, *De Officiis* 1, 42

Work was, literally, a man's work. It would never have occurred to Caecilia to go out to work. Some women did, of course, make a career in the professions – we hear, for example, of secretaries, clerks and stenographers, writers, teachers, doctors and nurses, but these were comparatively rare and far outnumbered by male colleagues. Javolenus Priscus and Caecilia knew midwives and wet nurses through the birth of their children, and they were friends with a number of doctors. They knew of Antiochis, daughter of a doctor, and Diodotus, who was so highly appreciated for her medical expertise by the people of Tlos in Lycia that they set up a statue celebrating her.

Where it was inappropriate for a man to do the work then women did come into their own: obvious examples are women's hairdressers, midwives, and seamstresses. Further down the social ladder, we hear of fishwives, costermongers, seamstresses, dressmakers, silk merchants, and distributors of wool.

If he wanted to appreciate the vast range of occupations at work in Rome then Javolenus Priscus need go no further than the nearest burial ground. We get an idea of the vast range of occupations taken by both men and women from funerary inscriptions; this selection is fairly typical: Publius Marcus Philodamus, construction worker; Quintus Tibertinus Menelaus who made a living slaughtering animals for sacrifices; Basileus who

Late first century/early second century AD. Women often shared in the running of the family business. This relief shows what is probably the potter's wife helping out in the production of some pots. The man is glazing while the woman holds a palm fan and a piece of bread, symbolizing her domesticity. The characters were almost certainly freedman and woman, possibly brought to Rome with the numerous slaves who came as skilled craftsmen after Rome's conquests of Greece and Spain. With permission from Virginia Museum of Arts, Richmond, Adolph D. and Wilkins C. Williams Fund; VA (object No. 60.2).

came to Rome from Bithynia Nikaia to teach mathematics and geometry.[1] We can add a nine-year-old worker in gold and a twenty-five-year-old shorthand writer in Greek, Hapate[2] and Thymele, trader in silk (ILS 7600), and nineteen-year-old Turia Privata, mime artist.[3] (ILS 5215).

Javolenus Priscus recalls how he saw a play by Plautus in which Megadorus bemoans the crowds of suppliers delivering and collecting payment:

> There stands the launderer, the embroiderer, the goldsmith, the wool-weaver, fringe makers, dealers in lingerie, crimson dyers, violet dyers, wax colour dyers, sleeve makers or perfumers, wholesale linen drapers, shoemakers, slipper-makers; sandal-makers stand there; stainers all stand there; cleaners make their demands, bodice-makers and apron-makers stand there. Just when you think you've got rid of them along comes three hundred more... weavers, lace-makers, cabinet-makers all turn up and the money's paid ... the dyers in saffron arrive.

Plautus, *Pot of Gold* 505-22

Woman poet, writer, or bookkeeper? *The Sappho* is in the Naples Archaeological Museum.

Martial's description of some urban development that has uncluttered the streets of Rome would have been instantly recognisable to Javolenus Priscus as his litter-bearers negotiated the crowds and clutter:

> That chancer of a hawker has robbed us of our Rome so that there are no longer any doorways on the doorways. Germanicus [Domitian], you have ordered that our narrow alleyways be widened and that what were once tracks become streets. None of the pillars [on the wine shops] are encircled by chained bottles any more[11] and the praetor doesn't have to work mired in mud; no one flashes a blade at random in the dense crowd and the dingy take-away doesn't take up the whole street. Barber, innkeeper, cook, butcher, all stick to their own doorways. Now Rome is Rome again – not just one great big shop.
>
> Martial 7, 61

A butcher chopping meat. Second century AD, Museo della Civiltà Romana, Rome.

To Juvenal, though, the *Subura* – a low-rent part of Rome Javolenus Priscus and his retinue sometimes passed through – was living hell; vivid description apart, Juvenal also demonstrates just how fortunate and privileged Romans like Javolenus Priscus were with their big houses and litters:

Subura – a place so wretched and desolate but better than living in fear of fires, buildings falling down all the time and a thousand other dangers in this savage Rome – with its bloody poets reciting all through August... In Rome most of the sick die from insomnia: the languor itself is caused by undigested food clinging to a peptic stomach. What lodgings let you sleep? Only the very rich can sleep in Rome and here lies the root cause of the urban malaise. The constant criss-crossing of wagons in the narrow winding streets, the drovers shouting out loud when their herds are jammed up ... When duty calls the rich man is carried through the yielding crowd and in a huge Liburnian galley rides roughshod over their heads. On the way he reads or writes or sleeps (closed windows make you sleepy in a litter). But even though we hurry, he gets there before us because that tide of humanity up ahead gets in the way and the great queue behind us crushes my groin. One man smacks me with his elbow, another thwacks me with a hard litter pole, but this one smashes a piece of wood, this one a jar, against my head. My legs are splattered with mud and it's not long before great big feet trample on me from all sides and a soldier stamps on my toe with his hobnail boots. Newly patched tunics are torn, a tall fir tree wobbles on an oncoming cart, other wagons carry a pine tree tottering menacingly above the crowds. If that axle carrying Ligurian marble should snap it will unleash an avalanche on the queues of people. What would be left of their bodies? Who will be able to find the body parts, the bones? All the corpses are indiscriminately crushed and perish just like the soul.

Juvenal, *Satires* 3

Slaves apart, for most Romans the working day lasted for six, seven or eight hours depending on the time of year; it was all over by the seventh hour. Shops opened at dawn but closed well before sunset; taverns and brothels, of course, stayed open until the last customer left the premises.

Javolenus Priscus, or rather his litter bearers, struggled on and eventually reached their destination and the day's cases, held today in the Basilica Julia on the south side of the Imperial Forum. Julius Caesar dedicated the Basilica in 46 BC and paid for it from his prodigious Gallic War booty; it was completed by Augustus, who named the building after Caesar, his adoptive father.

The Basilica was home to the civil law courts; some *tabernae* (shops), government offices and banks rented space here too. It was also was used for sessions of the *Centumviri* (Court of the Hundred), who presided over matters of inheritance. Not all cases were held here though; it was quite common for cases to be heard in private houses or even out in the open air in the Forum.

Notes

1. CIL 9, 1721; 1, 1604; IGUR 1176.
2. ILS 7760.
3. ILS 7600, ILS 5215.

Choregos and actors mosaic. Naples National Archaeological Museum. From the House of the Tragic Poet (VI, 8, 3), Pompeii.

CHAPTER VI

GOING SHOPPING

Now that she was made-up, coiffured, and dressed, Caecilia Priscus decided that a spot of shopping was in order, accompanied as usual by two female slaves and a parasol to deflect the beating sun.

Dressmakers, jewellers, perfumers and gift shops were the target; the slaves did the food shopping, or Javolenus who also collected the bread dole. Caecilia would attend to the children and the other slaves when she got back.

Rome was the centre of the empire and it boasted a shopping experience to end all shopping experiences; Caecilia could only agree with Martial that the city was one big shop, and long may it remain. She also agreed with the old historian Livy when he reported at the beginning of the century (34.7) in relation to the 195 BC repeal of the *Lex Oppia* – sumptuary laws targeting women's luxury:

Women cannot hold magistracies, priesthoods, celebrate triumphs, wear badges of office, enjoy gifts, or booty. Elegance, finery, and beautiful clothes are women's emblems; this is what they love and are proud of, this is what our ancestors called women's decoration.

Out shopping. This French postcard from the 1920s shows a group of well-to-do Roman women out shopping (and flirting) in a busy street. Note the old, not-so-wel-off lady in the bottom right corner selling her vegetables. The painting, *Dans la Rue*, hangs in the Petit Palais, Musée des Beaux-Arts de la Ville de Paris.

Mercatus Traiani (Trajan's Market), a semicircular market in Rome built by Apollodorus of Damascus in 110 CE. Image courtesy of photographer Elias Z. Ziadeh. This complex housed a whole market within its premises, along with small shops in the front and a residential apartment block. Trajan's Market had more than 150 shops in what was one of the first shopping centres.

Shops, market traders, street sellers and hawkers were everywhere: around temples, bathhouses, the forums, the Circus Maximus, amphitheatres and theatres. Street food was all over the place too, with countless stalls, their smells and aromas and delicacies from all over the empire: breads, sausages, pastries, and chickpeas were just what the busy Roman needed.

A shoe seller marks out his pitch next to bread and vegetable sellers on wooden trestles and in baskets on the ground. There are cages of chickens and hares, bowls of figs, and a barrel full of snails. Two monkeys clambering all over a stall have been trained to attract and stay customers.

The noise is deafening – a constant cacophony of shouts, cries, and bellowing. Seneca complains about the din from the hawkers who mob the bathhouse below his flat, describing the racket from the 'pastry-cooks shouting this and yelling that, the seller of sizzling sausages and the sweet shop man and all the fast food men and women from the cook shops selling their hearts out for all they have to sell'.

Martial compares the wit of a friend to that of a 'vendor of boiled chickpeas', or the slaves of the fishmongers, or the 'bawling cook who sells smoking sausages in stuffy bistros'. The *macellum* – a purpose-built luxury food market – was the place to go for fish, where single fish were auctioned off to the highest bidder. Red mullet was an expensive favourite; so much so that bankers sidled up to lend money to those who ran out of cash. There were also various meats for sale, some of which was fresh from animal sacrifices: beef, goat, pork, mutton, poultry, even swan; other delicacies on offer included songbirds, dormice, and snails.

For Caecilia, December was the best shopping month because that's when the Romans celebrated the festival of Saturnalia in honour of the god Saturn. They threw off their formal togas and spent their time eating and drinking and shopping. Juvenal writes that women, always desperate to outdo each other, threw caution to the wind and bought crystal vases and diamond rings from the stalls in the market in the *Porticus Argonautarum*. This is just what attracted Caecilia most.

Chapter VII

Keeping The Law

Javolenus Priscus had a full day ahead of him at the Basilica; as with most other days his civil law cases would take him right up to the fourth hour,[1] if not until sunset, as laid down in about 450 BC by the Twelve Tables.[2]

Pliny was later to note in one of his letters that Javolenus was a noted specialist in civil law, if something of an eccentric.[3]

The Romans were getting more and more litigious. Litigation was swamping the courts. Augustus in 2 BC was forced to allow his forum to be used for court hearings, such was the increasing volume and need for over-spill accommodation. More recently, Vespasian had despaired of the fact that the 'life of the advocates could hardly suffice' to deal with the number of law suits.[4] In Javolenus' time, civil cases were heard on 230 days of the year, while criminal cases took place on all 365 days – all were attended by a mob of public spectators although, obviously, the more salacious criminal cases drew the larger crowds.

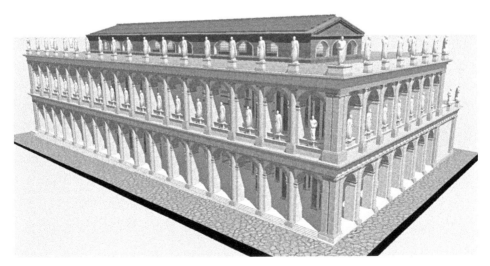

A 3D, computer-generated image of the Basilica Julia by Lasha Tskhondia. The Basilica was built in 46 BC by Julius Caesar in the Forum.

A famous old Roman trial: Cicero vs the conspirator Catiline. Originally published in *A Comic History of Rome.*

Javolenus got out of his litter on the Via Sacra and went up the seven steps of the Basilica to the marble portico and into the great hall with its three naves separated by thirty-six marble-faced columns. Above, in a large public gallery sat the spectators, men and women. The Centumviral Court comprised four courts, or chambers, made up of members of the *centumviri* – legal inflation had swelled their numbers from 100 to 180. These courts each comprised forty-five *centumviri* under the authority of a *decemvir*. When the Centumviral Court sat as one, ninety *centumviri* were involved. The four courts were separated by a curtain or screen so noise pollution from the other courts was a constant problem. Javolenus always remembered with a smile the time when, around twelve years ago in AD 68, Galerius Traculus with booming voice had been applauded by the audiences of all four courts, although three of the courts could not see him and should not have been able to hear him.[5]

Javolenus, at least, was relieved that he would not have to deal with the 'rent-a-mob' professional hecklers whom some lawyers engaged to help them win cases by simply causing disruption, bribing the public gallery to applaud and making a general nuisance of themselves.[6] It all started about ten years ago with Larcius Licinus but came to a head one day when Domitius Afer was speaking, only to be interrupted by loud applause in one of the other courts. When Afer learned that it was Licinus next door, he gave up on his case and declared his profession to be dead on its feet.

Membership of the *centumviri* was one of the first steps on the *cursus honorum* – the ladder of civil and military posts climbed by men of the senatorial class. Contested wills and inheritance issues formed a large part of the court's work; this is where Javolenus' expertise lay. Cicero, Tacitus and Pliny the Younger had all declaimed in the Centumviral Court.

Javolenus' particular *cursus* had already taken in two legionary commands; he had been a legal assessor (*iuridicus*) in Britannia. He was later to be consul in AD 86, governor of Germania in AD 90, and then governor of Syria and *proconsul* of Africa. He was part of the Sabinian Law School and edited works on Antistius Labeo, among others. He himself was the author of fifteen books of letters that addressed challenging legal problems.

Notes

1. See Martial 8, 57, 3.
2. Gellius 17, 2, 10; *Twelve Tables* 1, 6.
3. Pliny, Letters, 6, 15, 3.
4. Suetonius, *Vespasian* 10.
5. Quintilian, *Institutio Oratoria* 12, 5, 6.
6. Pliny, *Letters* 2, 14, 9.

Cicero Denounces Catiline (1889) by Cesare Maccari, in the Palazzo Madama, Rome.

CHAPTER VIII

HOME EDUCATION AND GOING TO SCHOOL

As *matrona* of the household, Caecilia had a number of clearly defined responsibilities. She had to 'work the wool', keep the family in decent clothes, she had to manage the household – including the slaves and the household budget, to look after the family and household gods, and she had to attend to the education of her children.

In reality, much of the work around the house was delegated to the slaves, as was the needlework – working the wool was more symbolic than anything else these days. The gods were no problem and much of her responsibilities for education diminished as the children got older.

In the olden days, Roman children were educated at home by father and mother and perhaps a literate slave. The aim was to imbue in the child life skills and a solid grounding in writing, reading, and numbers, which would furnish him or her to take their place in society as good Roman citizens, equipped with all the necessary virtues: respect and duty (*pietas*) to family, Rome, and the gods, as well as diligence, industriousness, and ambition. However, in more recent times, a more formal education system had developed with a broader curriculum and, for the boys at least, more focus on preparation for the *cursus honorum* – that political and military road map of service to the state.

So, from Vespasian's time (AD 69), the state was taking more responsibility for education: state-funded rhetoricians and *grammatici* in both Greek and Latin were beginning to emerge. Primary schools (*ludi*) were staffed by a magister or *litterator* and covered elementary education; secondary schools (*schola*), from around age twelve, were under a *grammaticus* and taught literature, Greek, and public speaking.

Suetonius records that there were twenty schools in Rome teaching grammar by the end of the Republic; Quintilian favoured schools to home tuition for the children of the elite.[1]

Caecilia knew that her children were privileged and lucky. For the children of the lower orders there was little education of any sort. The *litterator* stage was as far as it went. Boys had to work the land or help in the family business; they would often automatically follow in their fathers' occupation, receiving on-the-job training from an early age. Alternatively, a young boy would be contracted into an apprenticeship whereby he received no pay and lots of work; board and lodge were his only reward, with the hoped-for proficiency in a trade or manual job. Many boys joined the army.

Young girls also followed a trade sometimes, as these two epitaphs attest:

> In memory of Viccentia, a lovely girl, a worker in gold; she lived nine years.
>
> CIL 6, 9213

> In memory of Pieris, a hairdresser, she lived nine years
>
> CIL 6, 9731

Before Rome developed its own literature, Roman education was essentially Greek education. Until the Romans could provide their own critical mass of poetry and rhetoric written in Latin, all education was based on Greek works. Julius and Octavia, however, were fortunate to have a canon of literature to work on, providing gold standards in rhetoric, poetry, prose, and drama: Cicero and Virgil, Ovid and Terence, Livy and Lucretius, Gallus and Tibullus, to name but a few. Julius and Octavia's early education was delivered by a *litterator* or a magister (*ludi litterarii*) from around age seven; the goal was to perfect self-expression, knowing how to speak properly in public and to interpret the poets were essential skills. Painstaking and laborious work on the alphabet, first with letters, then with syllables, were the order of the day. Caecilia often supplemented the work of the *litterator*.

From age eleven, the education of Julius and Octavia went separate ways. For Julius, the *grammaticus* took over and the equally painstaking reading and analysis of literary texts began. Julius studied these less as an end in themselves and more as further preparation for his potential role as an orator in the courts or in the senate – something his father was keen to realise. Aptitude in public speaking was for many the be-all and end-all; it was the job of the *grammaticus* and then the *rhetor* to turn out a stream of adept public speakers. Julius studied subjects such as astronomy, music, philosophy, and natural science; literary criticism, geography, mythology, and grammar were also on what was a very crowded curriculum.

A description of a schoolboy's typical day tells us that Julius probably went home for lunch: 'I ate some white bread, olives, cheese, dried figs and nuts, I drank cold water and went back to school.'[4]

Lessons in rhetoric, under the *rhetor*, came next for fifteen-year-old Julius, bringing him yet closer to competence in public speaking and closer to the initial parts of the *cursus honorum*. Julius would soon discard his *toga praetexta* and don the *toga virilis*: his first stage of the *cursus honorum*. He would not pursue the *tirocinium militia* (military cadetship), but rather the *tirocinium fori* (legal apprenticeship) for a year – hopefully complemented by a gap year and some philosophy on a 'grand tour' of Greece or to a Greek colony such as Massilia.

Julius' father encouraged him to hang around the courts and listen to the orators and lawyers of the day, just as he had done himself, and Cicero before him.[2] Listening to, watching, and mixing with the experts was the way to success. Some twenty-two years later in AD 102, this advice still held up, according to Tacitus [3]. Once the basics had been mastered, Julius would move on to case studies: *suasoriae* were exercises in which a speech was created to persuade an individual to take a particular course of action; *controversiae* were speeches arguing one side of a point of law.[5]

Above left: Relief found in Neumagen near Trier, a teacher with three *discipuli*. *Circa* AD 180–185. Photo by Shakko of a casting in the Pushkin Museum, Moscow.

Above right: Roman bronze statuette after a Hellenistic model, showing a young girl reading. Cabinet des Médailles. (© Marie-Lan Nguyen)

Meanwhile, eleven-year-old Octavia was at home being schooled by Caecilia, in her role as *materfamilias*. This was chiefly instruction and practice in domestic duties – essentially working the wool and keeping the house – in preparation for her role as *matrona*. For Octavia this eventuality could loom into her life anytime from the age of twelve – next year! From then on it was, hopefully, a succession of pregnancies producing babies – ideally boys for the next generation of lawyers and soldiers.

Because women were largely excluded from public life there was little or no need to instruct them in rhetoric and declamation. Marriage, too, was a limiting factor: when a girl married at twelve or thirteen, the fledgling *matrona* had little time for education; her concern would soon be the education of the children she was expected to produce. Some young women did of course, in the richer families, move on to the grammar stage.

The school that Julius attended was very much an ad hoc affair in a rented room in an apartment block; sometimes in the summer it was al fresco, with lessons conducted on the pavement amid the noise and chaos of traffic and shoppers. As we know from a grumpy, sleep-deprived Martial, an early start was essential if the worst of the cacophony was to be avoided.[6]

Rote learning and corporal punishment were rife. Indeed, Julius observed that little had changed since the schooldays of Horace (65 BC – 8 BC), whom he recalls writes about the parrot fashion recitation of epic poetry of Livius Andronicus, drummed into him by *plagosus* Orbilius – Orbilius the flogger.[7] Suetonius provides some detail:

> Lucius Orbilius Pupillusa of Beneventum was left alone in the world by the death of his parents … when he had completed his military service, he resumed his studies … After teaching for a long time in his native town, he eventually went to Rome when he was fifty years old … where he taught, winning a greater reputation than any reward. In one of his books he admits that he was poor and lived in a garret. He also wrote a book called Perialogos, full of the wrongs which teachers suffered from the indifference or selfishness of parents. Indeed Orbilius was bad tempered, not only towards rival scholars whom he attacked at every opportunity, but also with his pupils, as Horace implies when he calls him "the flogger", in the line: "Whoever Orbilius thrashed with cane or with leather whip." He was even rude to distinguished men; when he was unknown and was giving testimony in a crowded court-room, when asked by Varro Murena, the lawyer on the other side, what he did and what his profession was, he replied: "I take hunchbacks from the sun and put them into the shade." Murena was a hunchback.
>
> Suetonius, *On Grammarians* 9

Needless to say, Julius agreed with the more enlightened Quintilian, who said:

> I do not approve of flogging, although it happens all the time; first, it is a shameful form of punishment and is fit only for slaves; it is insulting … Secondly, if a boy is so opposed to being taught that being rebuked is pointless, he will, like the worst type of slave, merely become inured to the blows. Finally, there would be absolutely no need for such punishment if the teacher were a good disciplinarian.
>
> Quintilian, *Institutio Oratoriae* 1, 3, 13–14

Notes

1. Suetonius, *On Grammarian*s 3; Quintilian, *Institutio Oratoria* 1, 2.
2. Cicero, *Brutus* 305–16.
3. Tacitus, *Dialogus de Oratoribus* 34, 1–6.
4. *Corpus Glossariorum Latinorum* III, pp. 645–7.
5. For a famous example of a *suasoria* see Seneca the Elder, *Suasoriae* 3, 6, 7; for a *controversia*, Seneca the Elder, *Controversiae* 1, 2.
6. Martial 9, 68 1–4, 8–12.
7. Horace, *Epistles* 2, 1, 70–71.

CHAPTER IX

SLAVE LABOUR

Slavery was another essential facet of life in ancient Rome. Slaves were crucial to the smooth running of Roman society, commerce, industry, war, public administration and education.

The more Rome conquered, the more slaves poured into Rome and other Italian towns and cities, and into the very foreign cities that Rome conquered and Romanised around the empire. War victims – women and children – and prisoners of war and deserters were the main source of supply, but there were others, including those unfortunates kidnapped and ransomed off by pirates, political and common criminals, debtors, abandoned or exposed children, and the children of slaves. By Javolenus' time, up to thirty per cent of the population of Rome comprised people in servitude.

There were more household slaves than any other kind. However, some were state-employed, building and maintaining public buildings, and running public services. Others were essential in keeping the water flowing in towns and cities, and the aqueducts and sewers working. Some were bought or hired to haul all manner of loads and freight from one place to another, and to drive carts, loading and unloading deliveries. At the lowest end, some were enlisted as gladiators to fight in the arena, often to the death, or as fodder for wild animals in the arena, ending in mutilation and death. Others still were bought as prostitutes, freaks, or even pets. Farm slaves were probably worse off in many ways than city slaves, as agricultural work was physically draining and their absent masters delegated control to slave overseers who would have been extremely demanding just to keep their jobs. A farm slave was barely higher than the farm animals in the agricultural labour food chain; a standing threat in Roman comedy was 'I'll send you to work on the farm!'

Hard labour in the lucrative silver mines was particularly brutal:

The slaves who work in [the silver mines] produce for their taskmasters revenues beyond belief, but in doing so they exhaust their bodies day and night in their excavations, dying in droves due to the exceptionally bad treatment they endure. There is no respite or break from their work... indeed to them death is preferable to life, such is the enormity of the hardships they must endure.

Diodorus Siculus 5, 38, 1

Right: Statue of a mourning barbarian woman; a victim of war, almost certainly destined for a life of servitude. It stands in the Loggia dei Lanzi in Florence. It was originally thought to be Thusnelda, wife of the captured Arminius but is probably a personification of Germania. A. W. Lawrence described the statue's 'intensity of grief' in his *Classical Sculpture*.

Below: The road back to Rome with its rotting trail of crucified supporters of Spartacus after their defeat by a vengeful Crassus. The painting, *The Crucified Slaves* (1878), is by Fyodor Andreyevich Bronnikov (1827–1902) and hangs in the Tretyakov Gallery in Moscow.

Mill work was no better; here the life of the slaves was unspeakably atrocious:

> Good God, what pathetic slaves they were! Some had skin black and blue all over
> from the beatings, some had their backs striped with lashes merely covered rather
> than clothed with torn rags, some had their groins barely concealed by a loin cloth;
> so ragged were they that they might as well have been naked; some were branded
> on the forehead; some had their hair shaven; some had shackles on their ankles;
> their skin was an ugly sallow; some could barely see, their eyes and faces were so
> black with the smoke, their eye-lids all glued up with the gloom of that fetid place,
> half blind and sprinkled black and white with dirty flour like boxers.
>
> Apuleius, *Metamorphoses* 9, 12

Slave owners could get away with such treatment because slaves were invisible in the
eyes of the law. Slaves had no rights; they were merely their owners' property, no more
than living labour-saving machines. Misconduct or alleged criminal activity could lead
to crucifixion or being burned alive. Psychological torture was applied when an owner
threatened to sell off a slave's spouse or children to another owner. It took until the Law
Code of Theodosius in AD 438 for this repellent practice to be repealed.

It comes as no surprise that some slaves did rise up and revolt. In 134 BC there was
an insurrection of slaves at the Laurium silver mines in Attica. Attalus, the heirless king
of Pergamum, bequeathed his state to Rome to prevent a simmering slave revolt. In
Lydia in AD 399, hordes of slaves joined the Ostrogoth army. Slaves plundered Thrace
in AD 401. In the siege of Rome by the Goths in AD 408–09, most of Rome's slaves –
40,000 in all – went over to the Goths.

The first major uprising became known as the First Servile War (135–132 BC); it
began on a large farm owned by a Greek from Henna, called Damophilius. In 136 BC,
Eunus, a slave from Apamea in Syria occupied Henna (modern Enna) in central Sicily
with 400 other runaways. It was not until 132 BC when slave-occupied Messina fell to
the Romans that the slave army was defeated and either re-enslaved or crucified.

As noted above, one of the ways in which slaves could generate income was by
training them as gladiators – or as wild animal fodder in gladiatorial conquests. A lot of
money could be made here, particularly with the celebrity status won among the more
successful survivors and veterans of the arena. One such celebrity was a slave by the
name of Spartacus.

Gladiatorial contests were serious business. The gladiators had to be good if the
baying crowds that flocked to the shows all around the empire were to go home satisfied.
Gladiators underwent training in gladiatorial schools. In 73 BC, seventy-eight of them
escaped from the fighting school of Gnaeus Lentulus Batiatus at Capua. According to
Plutarch, the gladiators at this point were only armed with meat cleavers and spits stolen
from the kitchen, but as luck had it, they came upon a wagon filled with gladiatorial
weaponry. Now heavily armed, they occupied a slope on Mount Vesuvius.

Despite a series of initial successes, Spartacus was ultimately defeated. The Romans
captured 6,000 of his unfortunate fellow slaves alive. As a stark, rotting reminder of
the fate that awaited the rebellious slave they were all crucified on crosses placed every
forty metres or so along the 150 miles of the Via Appia between Rome and Capua;
the corpses were slowly eaten away by wild dogs and carrion. Pompey butchered a

further 5,000 'survivors'. By contrast, 3,000 Roman prisoners of war were liberated at Spartacus's camp at Rhegium, alive and well.

Slaves provoked widely diverging attitudes. Martial's defence of his brutish treatment of his cook (8, 23) betrays what seems to be the standard attitude towards the servile classes. Cato had taken Aristotle's description of slaves as 'human tools' very literally and ill treatment of slaves was clearly endorsed by Quintillian (1, 3, 13–14): 'flogging is shameful, fit only for slaves.' However, it was not just the odd flogging, things could be much worse: eye-gouging, branding, limb smashing, and psychological and sexual abuse were seemingly all quite common. In addition, both female and male slaves often had to endure rape on a regular basis. Martial (3, 94) accuses Rufus of preferring to cut up his cook rather than the hare on his plate. In law, if a slave murdered his master then all of the household slaves (including women and children) were guilty by association (innocent or not) and executed along with the murderer.

But there was some enlightened, humane behaviour towards slaves and freedmen, as these tombstone epitaphs attest:

Some masters made their slaves part of the family:

> Gaius Calpenius Hermes built this tomb for himself and his children and his freedmen and freedwomen, and for his wife Antistia Coetonis.
>
> (CIL 14, 4827).

Some slave owners admired and appreciated their freedmen:

> Here lies Marcus Canuleius Zosimus; he was twenty-eight years old. His master erected this to a well-deserving freedman. In his lifetime he never spoke ill of anyone; he did nothing without his master's consent, there was always a lot of my gold and silver in his possession but he never stole any of it. He was a skilled master of Clodian engraving.
>
> (CIL 6, 9222.)

Javolenus shudders every time he remembers how Pliny describes in a letter to Acilius what must be every master's nightmare – being murdered by your slaves:

> Larcius Macedo – a man of praetorian rank – has suffered at the hands of his slaves. Admittedly, he was a bullying master and a thug who often forgot that his own father had been a slave – or perhaps he remembered it all too well? He was bathing in his villa at Formiae. Suddenly his slaves surrounded him. One grabbed him by the throat, another punched him in the face, another in his chest and stomach and even (and this is shocking to say) his balls. When they believed him to be dead they threw him out onto the baking hot patio to ensure that he was not still alive. Whether he was actually senseless or he just pretended to be so, Macedo lay there motionless and flat out to give the impression that he was dead. He was then carried out [by the slaves] to make it look as though he had been overcome by the heat. The slaves who had remained loyal to him picked him up; his concubines came running, wailing and bawling. Woken up by their shouting and by the cool

air, he opened his eyes and moved about to show that he was alive (now that it was safe to do so). The slaves who had revolted had scattered in all directions; most of them have been caught while the others are still being hunted. Macedo revived for a few days but it was a struggle: he died.

Pliny, Letters 3, 14

Seneca would appear to have the last word as published in AD 65, words that Javolenus likes to think he takes to heart:

> Kindly remember that he whom you call your slave sprang from the same stock, is smiled upon by the same skies, and on equal terms with yourself breathes, lives, and dies. It is just as possible for you to see in him a free-born man as for him to see in you a slave … I do not wish to involve myself in too big a question, and to discuss the treatment of slaves, towards whom we Romans are excessively haughty, cruel, and insulting: but this is the nub of my advice: treat your inferiors as you would be treated by your betters. And as often as you reflect how much power you have over a slave, remember that your master has just as much power over you.

Seneca, Moral Letters to Lucilius 47, 1–11

Enslavement was not always a life sentence. The Roman practice of *manumission* – setting a slave free – provided some slaves not just with yearned for liberty but also with Roman citizenship, social and financial independence, and in some rare cases high office in Roman administration, or even a place in the emperor's bed.

Slaves could buy their freedom if they saved up enough money from gifts and tips, or through bribes if in public service, or from even what they could steal; they would then repay the master the original price he paid or something deemed reasonable. Once released, the freedman would sometimes become the ex-owner's client, showing him loyalty and doing a specified number of days work for him each year. They might continue doing the same work they did as a slave, but with the crucial difference that they were now paid, and had to feed and clothe themselves.

The Priscus family kept a modest six slaves. They were all fourth generation, three men and three women, descendants of slaves all captured by Julius Caesar when he took more than a million slaves in his campaigns in Gaul between 58 and 51 in the previous century. Slaves contributed to and helped out in all aspects of the Priscus' family life. We have seen how they rose before dawn to get the household ready for the day. From then on they variously set about cleaning and maintaining the house. Juvenal in Satire 3 describes some of what routinely goes on: they wash the dishes, blow on the cooking flame and clatter the oily skin scrapers, lay out the towels, and fill the flasks. The slaves are hurrying about their various chores or helping Caecilia get dressed and made-up, chaperoning her in the city, sewing new clothes and mending, making the bread, occasionally escorting Javolenus to the baths, preparing, serving and clearing up after the evening meal, and securing the house when the family had retired for the night.

By Caecilia's time, though, things were beginning to change quite markedly. Lucius Junius Moderatus Columella, the Spanish-born writer on agriculture and husbandry, complains that homespun clothes were now unfashionable and clothing was routinely bought from shops at extortionate prices.[1] Bread-making suffered the same fate as bakeries and bakers' shops gradually replace home-made bread. Indeed, Aelius Aristeides tells us that only in the poorest households did women do routine housework – slaves did most, if not all, of it.² On the catering front, the *materfamilias* was heavily involved, but only in a managerial capacity in the preparation and serving of meals.³

The wealthier Roman woman like Caecilia would spend much of her time supervising the slaves, ensuring that they performed all the mundane tasks, which, as we have noted, only a lower class housewife might be expected to do. This freed the *matrona* up to go out: shopping, attending festivals and spectacles, visiting friends, educating her children, and going to those dinner parties Nepos tells us about: 'What Roman is ashamed to bring his wife along to a feast?' Nowadays, Columella laments that women are obsessed with luxury and laziness; the making of wool has ceased and country women moan when they have to look after the farm just for a few days.

Slaves had a key role in the education of a master's children, helping the *materfamilias* or, depending on her education, taking over completely. Quintilian, with an eye on later skills in declamation, is concerned about a child nurse's credentials, specifically in a boy's early education:

> Above all ensure that the child's nurse speaks correctly … without doubt the most important thing is that they should be of good character: but they should speak correctly as well. The child hears his nurse first and it is her words that he will first try to copy. We naturally retain best those things we learned as a child … do not, therefore, let the boy even in infancy get used to a way of talking he will later have to unlearn.
>
> Quintilian, *Institutio Oratoria* 1, 1, 4–5

Some children grew very attached to their nurses (often a slave) and formed enduring attachments. Pliny, for example, bequeathed his farm to his nurse (*Letters* 6, 3).

Pedagogues were also important; they were the male slaves who played with, amused, and taught basic life skills to their young charges. They chaperoned young children from an early age to the baths and theatre. They did the school run, accompanying them to and from school. In essence, they were full-time babysitters. Cicero acknowledges their vital role while, at the same time, recommending that an appropriate distance be kept:

> Generally speaking, we should not make decisions about friendships until we are grown up and know our own minds. Otherwise our nurses and pedagogues – on the grounds that it is they who know us best – will lay claim to the best part of our affections. These people must not be neglected, but should be regarded differently from those friends we have made as grown-ups.
>
> Cicero, *On Friendship* 20, 74

Martial finds that some *pedagogues* will just not let go:

> As far as you're concerned [Charidemus] I still haven't grown up … you won't let me have a good time or go out with women … you tell me off, you watch me like a hawk, you complain and sigh and it takes you all your time to keep your angry hand off the birch. If I get dressed up in flash Tyrian clothes or slick back my hair

you exclaim "Your father never did that!" You … count every glass of wine I drink. Stop it! … my girlfriend will explain that I am a man now.

Martial 11, 39

Martial provides evidence that slaves were sometimes affectionately thought of. When he mourns the death of slave girl Erotion – his delight (*deliciae*) – just before her sixth birthday, he show *pathos* and deep grief. In the first of two poems, he hopes she will not be frightened by the horrors of Tartarus that await her, and that the turf over her body will not weigh too heavily; in the second, he asks for the anniversary of her death to be celebrated by subsequent owners of the house, where she lies buried:

> May little Erotion not be horrified by the black shades nor the many mouths of the Tartarean dog [Cerberus]. She would only have completed her sixth cold winter if she'd not lived as many days too few. Now, let her frolic and play with old friends, and chatter and lisp my name. May the spongy turf cover her soft bones: earth, lie lightly on her – she was never heavy on you.
>
> Here lies Erotion in the shade that too early descended, snatched away by criminal Fate in her sixth winter. Whoever you may be that, after me, rules over this little plot of land, bring annual devotions to her gentle shade. So … may this stone be the only one that is tearful on your land.

Martial, 5, 34; 10, 61.

On the other hand, Javolenus is appalled by the sadistic behaviour of Publius Vedius Pollio (d. 15 BC). Lampreys, trained to kill, brought out the worst in Pollio and the best in Augustus, his friend for a while. Whenever Vedius was irritated by his slaves he had them thrown into a pool of lampreys, which proceeded to tear the unfortunate victim to shreds. On one occasion, Vedius was about to despatch a slave who had accidentally broken a crystal cup, but Augustus, a guest, was so horrified that he halted the execution attempt and had all of Pollio's drinking vessels smashed to pieces. Augustus then went on to demolish Vedius' sumptuous villa, which he had inherited after the sadist's death.

The gods dealt a doubly devastating blow when a disabled person happened also to be a slave. There must have been many such unfortunates, due either to slaves being worked to within an inch of death, or through injuries sustained in battle before being consigned to servitude as war booty as a defeated prisoner of war. It seems likely that when a slave became too weak or disabled to be of any further practical use to his master, a 'useless mouth', he was simply killed. Claudius' law ruling that that disabled slaves should be abandoned rather than killed probably testifies to this. Freeing a disabled slave was probably the cruellest act of all – in effect, that slave was being consigned to a life in penury on the streets; it did, however, save the master money, which goes some way to explain its frequency.

Perhaps the most extraordinary, and untypical, story relating to a disabled person Javolenus has heard is left by Pliny the Elder when he describes what happened to the slave Clessipus, described by Pliny as 'an ugly hunchback' (*Natural History* 34, 11). A wealthy woman called Gegania went out shopping one day and decided to buy an expensive Corinthian chandelier for the prodigious sum of 50,000 sesterces; for good measure, the auctioneer threw in Clessipus as well, so she left the shop with a bronze candelabra and a slave with a deformity. Gegania showed him off at parties, and had him parade naked for the titillation of her guests. However, she also fell deeply in love with him, took him into her bed, and even changed her will to make him a beneficiary. On her death, Gegania's huge fortune came to Clessipus, who presumably spent the rest of his days giving thanks to the candelabra. Whether Clessipus was just a very clever fortune hunter we will never know.

There is even evidence that some sadistic Romans maimed their slaves deliberately, to create the grotesquely unusual in order to impress – a kind of perverted status symbol for the home that had everything. It seems that there was nothing like a dwarf, hunchback, manic depressive, blind, deaf, dumb, or blind man or woman to impress the neighbours or dinner guests. All of these exploited unfortunates were readily available from that special section of the slave market. Plutarch describes this hideous place, the τεράτων ἀγοράν (*teraton agora*) – 'monster market':

> Therefore, just as at Rome there are some who take no account of paintings or statues or even, by Heaven, of the beauty of the boys and women for sale, but haunt the monster-market, examining those who have no calves, or are weasel-armed, or have three eyes, or ostrich-heads, and searching to learn whether there has been born some commingled shape and malformed prodigy.
>
> Plutarch, *De Curiositate* 10 / *Moralia* 520c

An enlightened Longinus is yet more critical of this inhumane behaviour:

> And so, my friend adds, if what I hear is true, not only do the cages in which they confine the pygmies or dwarfs, as they are called, stunt the growth of their captives, but their bodies even shrink due to the close confinement, on the same principle that all slavery, however fair it may be, might be described as a cage for the human soul, a common prison.
>
> Longinus, *De Sublimitate* 44, 5

Every slave has his or her backstory, and will have been reduced to servitude for any number of reasons in any number of circumstances. Slavery could afflict anyone, often through no fault of his or her own: the educated, and the uneducated, the rich, the poor, young or old, man or woman, girl or boy. Here is a happy success story:

> Staberius Eros bought himself with his own savings at a public sale and was formally liberated because of his devotion to literature. He numbered Brutus and Cassius among his pupils. Some say that he was so noble that, in the times of Sulla, he admitted the children of the proscribed to his school free of charge.
>
> Suetonius, *On Grammarians* 13

Notes

1. Columella, praef 1–3; 7–9.
2. Aelius Aristides, Roman Oration 71b.
3. Petronius, Satyricon 37, 67.

CHAPTER X

TAKING CARE OF THE GODS

Women had a key role to play in religion, both domestic and, increasingly with the newer, exotic religions, public. When Caecilia married Javolenus she, in line with tradition, renounced her own religion and assumed her husband's; in other words, she adopted his gods and his ancestors.

Religion was something of a nightmare for women like Caecilia: she had to be familiar with all the relevant dates – when you could or could not do one thing or another. Marriage for Octavia was looming, and she would soon have to fix a date for the wedding, taking into account all the ineligible days. For example, there were certain days on which marriage ceremonies were avoided because they were deemed unlucky. *Calends, Nones,* and *Ides* were out because, as Varro tells us, the days after these were 'black days'; *Mundus Cereris*: the three days of the year (24 August, 5 October, and 8 November) when ghosts were afoot because the doors of Hades (*mundus*) gaped open; the *Lemuralia*: 9, 11 and 13 May devoted to celebrating the festival of the dead, hence, '*mense Maio malae nubent*' (they marry ill who marry in May); 18–21 February for similar reasons: the *Parentalia* in honour of family ancestors; May and early June because time was better spent farming the land, or because the cleaning of the temple of Vesta by the Vestal Virgins was not completed until 15 June; 1, 9, and 23 March were to be avoided because the dancing priests of Mars, the *Salii*, were moving the shields. In short, a wedding should take place on a happy day (*hilaris dies*).

One famous anecdote from the end of the second century BC made Caecilia shudder. It involved another Caecilia who was married to Metellus; she was anxious to find out from the gods what the future held for her betrothed niece so she and the niece took up post in a temple and waited for some news. The gods were reticent, until the bored niece asked to sit down next to her aunt. Her aunt innocently, but prophetically, invited her to take her place – and dropped down dead; the gods had taken her innocent offer literally. Metellus then married the niece. When dealing with the gods, extreme caution was always necessary and Caecilia was careful to watch what she asked the gods for – unlike her namesake.

Roman religion was built around a large and incestuous pantheon, in which the gods and goddesses governed and controlled everything that happened to Romans in their current life and in the next. Everyone had recourse and access to these divinities; they could be seen all around – painted on walls, erected in statuary, stamped on their coins, laid out

Detail of a *Lararium*:
House of Lucius, living
room. In the open-air
museum at Petronell,
Austria. Photographer
Wolfgang Sauber.

The oculus of the Pantheon
in Rome by night.

Jakob Alt (1789–1872):
*The Pantheon and
the Piazza della
Rotonda* (1836).

in mosaics on the floor. For those who could read they could learn all about them from, for example, Homer's *Odyssey*, Lucretius' *De Rerum Natura*, Cicero's *On the Nature of the Gods*, or Ovid's *Metamorphoses*. Theology or mythology could be read to the illiterate verbatim or communicated in stories. All Romans could see them on the stage, comedic or tragic, and the Roman would also see his or her divinities at countless festivals and in temples. In short, Roman gods were omnipresent and ubiquitous. Both Cicero and Virgil say so: 'God covers all things: the earth, the open seas and the vast skies'.[2]

Like many Romans, Caecilia found that state religion had become rather staid, dilapidated, and impersonal. Varro, in 47 BC, was so concerned by this decline and indifference that he wrote a book about Roman religion, lest it be forgotten. His *Human and Divine Antiquities* contains sixteen books describing the festivals, rites, priests, temples, divinities and institutions. Ovid, too, meticulously lists the various festivals and liturgies in his *Fasti*.

In Octavia's case, the state pantheon featured numerous deities dedicated to every conceivable aspect of a young teenage girl's life. Fortuna Virginalis looked after virgins and it was to her to whom girls turned and dedicated their togas when they reached physical and sexual maturity around the age of twelve, exchanging it for the *stola* – the garb of a *matrona*. Fortuna Primigenia of Praeneste followed marriage – the goddess of mothers and childbirth – whom women shared with men because she also was goddess of virility, material wealth, and financial success. Caecilia was careful to cultivate both divinities for Octavia's sake.

Official Roman religion was essentially founded on and catered for an agricultural society. For example, Jupiter made the crops grow with his rain and sun; Saturn encouraged sowing; Ceres promoted growth. As Rome's possessions increased and more of the world was 'Romanised', as Rome became more urbanised, then, with the syncretisation

A bronze Roman *lar* from around AD 50. Height: 22.5 cm (8.9 in). Width: 16 cm (6.3 in). Depth: 9 cm (3.5 in). In the National Archaeological Museum of Spain. Accession number 2943; discovered at Lora del Río, Seville.

of exotic and mysterious foreign gods and goddesses, traditional religion gradually lost much of its relevance to Roman life and culture. It became staid and unappealing, so men and women turned to and embraced the new, oriental, mystery religions, which they came into contact with as expansionists and conquerors when it percolated into Roman society. These cults – particularly the cult of Isis – offered women like Caecilia an active role in the priesthood; the cults could be personalised and customised to meet the needs of individuals, be they man or woman, and because their eschatology often enshrined birth and rebirth they offered hope of life after death; they promised immortality.

Bona Dea – the good goddess – emerged in Rome around 272 BC, during the Tarentine War; Bona Dea was associated with chastity and fertility and the protection of Rome; as Fauna she could prophesy the fates of women. She had two festivals: one at her temple on the Aventine, the other at the home of the *Pontifex Maximus* (chief priest). It was strictly women only.

The Bona Dea had a scandalous history that was still repeated in Caecilia's day. When the high-profile rites of 62 BC – hosted by Julius Caesar as that year's *Pontifex Maximus* – were infiltrated by a high-profile man, the ensuing scandal was huge; not least because Caesar's mother, Aurelia Cotta, Pompeia his wife, and his sister, Julia, and the Vestal Virgins were all there. According to Juvenal, any sexual propriety that remained in Rome evaporated that night. Publius Clodius Pulcher sacrilegiously gatecrashed the rites that were being held chez Caesar. Clodius had his eye on Pompeia and got dressed

Detail of a Roman *lararium* wall painting, Pompeii; exhibition at Europäischer Kulturpark Bliesbruck-Reinheim, 2007. Photographer Claus Ableiter.

up as a woman to enable himself to get close to her. The scandal led to Caesar distancing himself from and divorcing Pompeia: she was obviously implicated, and Caesar's wife must be above suspicion.

Other festivals flirted with by Caecilia included the *Terminalia*, a family affair that was originally celebrated at the limits of a Roman territory, or on the last day of the old Roman year. The *Lupercalia* took place in February: here women offered themselves up to be ritually whipped with goatskin to promote fertility, banish sterility, and ease childbirth. The Vestals handed out *mola salsa* – salted flour used in official sacrifices. It was sprinkled on the forehead, and between the horns of animal victims before they were sacrificed, as well as on the altar and in the sacred fire.

The temple of Carmenta may owe its origin to women who refused to sleep with their husbands pending the repeal of a law prohibiting them from riding in horse-drawn vehicles. Carmenta was the patroness of midwives; she invented the Roman alphabet. Women who sacrifice to Rumina (the goddess responsible for breastfeeding as the she-wolf that suckled Romulus) do so with milk and not wine because Rumina knows that alcohol is harmful to babies.

Rumina was by no means on her own. Alemona presided over the foetus and was akin to two of the *Parcae* (the Fates), Nona and Decima, responsible for the ninth and tenth months of gestation. Parca or Partula watched over the delivery; at the birth, Parca establishes the limit of the baby's life in her guise as a goddess of death called Morta.

The Atrium and Lararium. This is where the household and family gods – the *lares* and the *penates* – held sway in the bigger and wealthier Roman houses. Here we see the women and children of the house bringing offerings to the gods. The idealised scene is taken from a Liebig trade card issued by the Compagnie Liebig (later OXO), manufacturers of meat extracts with factories in Fray-Bentos in Uruguay and Colon in Argentina.

The *profatio Parcae* (prophecy of Parca) signalled the child as a mortal being; Vagitamus opens the baby's mouth to emit the first cry; Egeria brings out the baby. Postverta and Prosa avert breech birth, which was considered unlucky; Lucina is the goddess of the birth; Diespiter (Jupiter) introduces the infant to the daylight; Levana lifts the baby from the ground, symbolising contact with Mother Earth; Cunina looks after the baby in the cradle, protecting it from malevolent forces and magic; Statina gives the baby fitness; Candelifera keeps the nursery light burning to deter the spirits of darkness that would threaten the infant in the crucial first week of birth, and banishes the bogey-women – child-snatching demons such as Gello. On the *dies lustricus*, the *Fata Scribunda* were invoked. The Written Fates was a ceremonial inscription of the child's new name; the giving of a name was as important as the birth itself – receiving a *praenomen* established the child as an individual with its own fate. Potina allows the child to drink, Edusa to eat; Ossipago builds strong bones, Carna strong muscles, defending the internal organs from witches; Cuba is there to ease the child's transition from cradle to bed; Paventia deflects fear from the child; Peta attends to its first demands; Agenoria bestows an active life; Adeona helps it learn to walk. Iterduca and Domiduca watch over it as it leaves the house and returns home again; Catius Pater makes children clever; Farinus teaches children to talk; Fabulinus gives the child's first words; Locutius helps it to form sentences; Mens provides intelligence; Volumnus makes the child want to do good;

Io is carried by a river god, setting her down at Kanopus near Alexandria. Roman *fresco* from the temple of Isis in Pompeii. Museo Archeologico Nazionale, Naples.

Numeria is there for counting, Camena for singing; the Muses bestow an appreciation of the arts, literature, and sciences – and so it went on with a host of *indigitamenta* – spirits – or gods, attending every single stage of life, and death. All of this Caecilia would have to make Octavia aware of as her wedding draws ever closer.

An early, and officially sanctioned, import from Asia Minor was Cybele, or Magna Mater; she was a universal earth mother who looked out for all things maternal and represented rebirth and immortality through the resurrection of Attis. Cybele was brought to Rome in 204 BC after consultation of the Sibylline Books revealed that victory over the Carthaginians could be ensured by her presence.

Once the cult was established, however, the Roman authorities must have wished that they had taken more care over what they had wished for. The orgiastic, frenzied rites, the eunuchs, the dancing, the self-castration and other acts of self-harm by adherents – the *Galli* – were all quite alien and objectionable to establishment Romans. Measures were taken to control the cult and to marginalise it as far as possible.

For Caecilia, however, the oriental cult of Isis held the greatest appeal. It spread to Italy from Egypt at the end of the second century BC and had immediate appeal to women, not least because Isis was associated with a number of other more familiar

Altar of the twelve gods, perhaps the rim of a well or a Zodiac altar. The object represents the twelve gods of the Roman pantheon, each identified by an attribute: Venus and Mars linked by Cupid, Jupiter and a lightning bolt, Minerva wearing a helmet, Apollo, Juno and her sceptre, Neptune and his trident, Vulcan and his sceptre, Mercury and his *caduceus*, Vesta, Diana and her quiver, and Ceres. Marble, found in Gabii, Italy, first century AD. Louvre Museum.

female deities such as Athena, Aphrodite, Hera, Demeter, and Artemis. She was also seen as being caring and compassionate, devoting time to each of her initiates. Moreover, Isis was flexible and versatile; she was all things to all men, and all thing to all women. One inscription describes her perfectly: 'goddess Isis, you who are one and all.'³ She was a woman and a mother herself who had known grief and bereavement; she had been a prostitute in Tyre and therefore appealed to the whole range of female Roman society. She was beneficent and came to be associated with fertility – every year when she saw famine encroaching on Egypt, she wept in sorrow so that her tears replenished the Nile and irrigated the flood plains. She was responsible for the Egyptian practice of honouring queens above kings, as exemplified by Cleopatra; most crucially, she made the power of women equal to that of men.⁴ Women would have sympathised with Isis' role as a mother, depicted as she often is with a baby in her arms – Horus, the offspring of her incestuous relationship with Osiris, her brother. Death and resurrection could be recognised in the rejuvenated Egyptian lands and the death and rebirth of Osiris, also her husband.

Men and women of every age and rank were involved in the cult of Isis. At festivals the women, all dressed in white, sprayed their hair with perfume; they strew the road with flowers and perfumes, notably balsam, fixed mirrors on their backs to reflect Isis as she approached, and pretended to comb her hair with ivory combs.

The inclusiveness of the cult was what appealed to Caecilia. It set it apart from official Roman religion as it allowed women to aspire to high religious office and become priestesses. One inscription shows us six female Isis *sacerdotes* (out of twenty-six), one of which was a woman of senatorial rank, another the daughter of a freedman, Usia Prima.⁵ Around one third of Isis devotees mentioned in Italian inscriptions are women.

As the popularity of the cult spread and grew, so predictably did the official suspicion and paranoia. Augustus had seen in Isis a worrying reincarnation of Cleopatra and a

Side of a Roman sarcophagus showing the Dioscuri: Castor and Pollux and horses. It was found in a garden in Middlesbrough and presented to the Dorman Museum in the town by the Middlesbrough Temperance Society in 1926.

threat to his moral legislation. In 28 BC he banned the building of temples of Isis within the city of Rome and in 21 BC extended this to an exclusion zone outside the city.

The hearth was literally the focus of the Roman household, traditionally tended by the *matrona* and daughters of the family. *Lares* were guardian gods with an extensive remit covering roads, seas, agriculture, livestock, towns, cities, the state, and the army; they were all under the protection of their particular *lar* or *lares*. But one of its most important functions was as a god of the household. By extension, they became guardian gods of the domestic hearth; the statues of domestic *lares* took pride of place at the table during family meals and their presence and blessing were essential at all important family events, such as weddings, births, and adoptions. They were housed in a shrine along with the images of the household's *penates*, *genius*, and any other favourite deities, thus providing a religious focal point for social and family life. Individuals or families who neglected their *Lares* could expect bad luck.

The *Lares* were similar to the *di penates* or *penates* – household deities that were also invoked in most domestic ceremonies. When the family had a meal, they threw a morsel into the fire on the hearth for the *penates*. They were thus associated with Vesta (goddess of the hearth), the *lares*, and the *Genius* of the *paterfamilias* (master of the house). They were also gods of the storeroom or larder (*penus*), which was in the innermost part of the house; here they mounted guard over the household's food, wine, oil, and other staples and essentials. Because they were associated with the source of a family's food they came to symbolise the continuing life and sustainability of the family.

It was Caecilia's and Octavia's responsibility to manage the cultivation of the *lares* and *penates* in the Priscus household – a task delegated to them by Javolenus as the *paterfamilias*. So, part of the day was given over to keeping the hearth fire burning – a domestic version of the state responsibility of the Vestal Virgins – replenishing the *penus*, and looking after the *lares* and *penates* at mealtimes and at special occasions. They made various offerings of spelt wheat and grain-garlands, honey cakes and honeycombs, grapes and first fruits, wine, and incense. Any food that fell to the floor during meals or banquets was claimed by the *lares*.[6]

As noted, domestic *lares* were there at significant occasions in the life of a family. When he came of age, Julius would donate his personal amulet (*bulla*) to his *lares* before donning his manly toga (*toga virilis*). After the ritual shaving off of his first beard it was placed in their keeping. On the night before her wedding, Octavia would be giving up her dolls, soft balls, and breast bands to her family *lares*, as a sign that she had come of age. On her wedding day she will transfer her allegiance to her husband's neighbourhood *lares* (*lares compitalici*) by paying them a copper coin on the way to her new home. She paid another coin to her new domestic *lares*, and one to her husband. All of this had to be managed and organised by Caecilia.

Notes

  1. Varro, *De Lingua Latina* 6, 29 and Macrobius 1, 21.
  2. Cicero, *De Deorum Natura* 2, 70–72; Virgil, *Georgics* 4, 221ff.
  3. *CIL* 10, 3800.
  4. *P. Oxy* 11, 1380, 214–216.
  5. *CIL* 6, 224.
  6. Pliny the Elder, *Natural History*, 28, 27.

CHAPTER XI

A LETTER FROM THE EDGE OF EMPIRE

Javolenus Priscus had a younger brother who was in the Roman army; he was, of course, uncle to Julius and Octavia. Octavius Priscus was a Legion Legate in the IXth Hispana Legion based in Eboracum under Agricola, Imperial Legate and Governor of Britannia.

The IXth legion was about 5,500 men strong; the usual six military tribunes reported to Octavius as well as the commander of the camp and various staff officers in charge of engineers, stores, weapons, priests, musicians, medical support, and record keepers. The cavalry commanders also reported to him.

Twenty years or so earlier the legion had suffered serious casualties at the Battle of Camulodunum (modern Colchester) when Boudica, queen of the Iceni tribe, revolted against Roman rule.[1]

One way in which local tribes could guarantee peaceful co-existence with Rome was to bequeath to the Romans their lands on the death of the monarch. Prasutagus, prosperous king of the Iceni (inhabiting what is roughly today's East Anglia), did just that, citing Nero as heir but with an additional clause naming his daughters as co-heirs. The Iceni had been on friendly terms with the Romans since the early days of the invasion but on the king's death in AD 60 the Romans chose to ignore the small print in the king's will, took over the kingdom, and plundered it. Perhaps it was naive of the Iceni to expect an extension of the special relationship after Prasutagus' death but the aftermath of the Roman decision was shocking, brutal, and highly provocative: Prasutagus' daughters were raped, Queen Boudica, his wife, was flogged, the family was treated like slaves, and his Roman creditors called in their loans; loans that the Iceni had been led to believe were gifts. Boudica was humiliated and outraged.

At the time, Gaius Suetonius Paulinus, the Roman governor, was preoccupied with trying to take Mona, Anglesey. The objective was to eradicate the exiled druid community there and end the island's status as a haven for disaffected refugees. Druidism was feared by the Romans, not least because of its reputation for focusing opposition to Roman rule and for their veneration of the human head, which led to routine decapitation of corpses after battle. This head-hunting can be seen depicted on Trajan's Column. According to Tacitus, the druids had a reputation for 'soaking their altars in the blood of prisoners and using human entrails in their divination' (human sacrifice in other words). Paulinus' soldiers lined up opposite an armed force, among which were 'women dressed in black robes with dishevelled hair like Furies, brandishing torches. Next to them were the druids, their hands

The Temple of Claudius in Camelodunum by Peter Froste (b. 1935), going up in flames at the hands of Boudica AD 60. (© Colchester and Ipswich Museums Service.)

raised to the skies, screaming fearsome curses'. The Romans were at first paralysed with fear but then attacked, slaughtered all before them, and hacked down the sacred groves.[2]

Elsewhere in Britannia the time was ripe for rebellion: in AD 61 the Iceni under Boudica advanced on the *colonia* of Camulodunum with its Temple of Claudius, a citadel symbolic of oppressive Roman rule. The Iceni were joined by the disaffected Trinovantes, the tribe that had been displaced and enslaved to make way for the *colonia*. The omens were not good for the Romans: 'the statue of Victory in Camulodunum crashed to the ground as if in flight; there were lamentations, though no mortal man had uttered the words or the groans'; hysterical women chanted impending doom, 'at night there was heard to issue from the senate-house foreign jargon mingled with laughter, and from the theatre more cries; a ghost town on the Thames was seen to be in ruins and the Channel turned blood red; shapes like bodies were washed up'.[3] More crucially, Camulodunum was not fortified and largely undefended – Suetonius Paulinus had fatefully posted the XXth legion to the Welsh borders. The *procurator* was found wanting: when the Roman inhabitants clamoured for reinforcements, Catus Decianus sent a mere 200 auxiliary troops.

Camulodunum was sacked and the temple fell after two days; the *saevitia* (savagery) of Boudica's forces was uncompromising. The IXth legion under Petillius Cerealis rushed to relieve the defenders but was annihilated. Catus Decianus fled to Gaul. Only the IXth's cavalry escaped to fight another day. The legion was later reinforced with legionaries from Germania. When Cerialis was posted back as governor of Britannia in AD 71 he took command of the IXth once more in a successful campaign against the Brigantes to subdue north and central Britain. Pride was restored and a new headquarters at Eboracum was built.[4]

By AD 80 Octavius Priscus and the IXth were in the front line, ready for Agricola's invasion of Caledonia. They had taken the Scottish lowlands and controlled the land between the Tyne-Solway and the Forth-Clyde isthmuses, inhabited by the Votadini and Selgovae, pushing as far north as the Tavus (the River Tay).[5] They had another lucky escape when, according to Tacitus, the Caledonians surprised the Romans in a night attack on their fort. The Caledonians burst in, striking panic amongst the Romans, and slaying the sentries, but Agricola sent his cavalry in to save the legion. The legion responded, took heart, and fought for their honour, repelling the Caledonians.[6]

Inspired by this success, the Romans pushed north for the decisive battle of Mons Graupius, near the Moray Firth.[7] Flushed by the success of the IXth Hispana, Octavius Priscus described the battle and its preamble in a letter to his brother, Javolenus, back in Rome:

Salve.

I pray to the Lares, the household gods of my present billet that I may find you and our whole family in good health.

    The news is that we have just defeated the Britons at the battle here at Mons Graupius, a godless and desolate place many miles from anything you could call civilisation. Our victory surely means that Britannia is now ours and we can get on with the business of Romanisation. Perhaps our next target will be Hibernia, a large island off the west coast.

You might like to know that in the centre our auxiliary infantry numbered 8,000 men flanked by 3,000 cavalry; the Roman legionaries were in front of their camp in reserve. Altogether our army was 23,000 men strong. The Caledonian army was led by a chieftain called Calgacus, 30,000 strong, some of whom were on higher ground rising up in tiers in a kind of horseshoe formation. Their chariots sped about in no man's land. Spears from both sides filled the air before Agricola ordered the auxiliaries to launch a frontal attack: four cohorts of Batavians and two cohorts of Tungrian swordsmen clashed with the Caledonians, stabbing them in the face; they were soon all cut down on the lower slopes of the hill. The enemy chariots were dealt with by our cavalry. An outflanking movement by the barbarians further up the hill failed when they themselves were outflanked by four squadrons of cavalry which Agricola had wisely held in reserve for just such an eventuality. The routed Caledonians fled into a nearby wood and were pursued mercilessly and relentlessly by Roman units. 10,000 Caledonians fell that day; we lost a mere 360 auxiliary troops. Our legions in reserve had no cause to intervene.

Will write again soon, perhaps from Hibernia.
Vale.
Octavius.

Notes

1. Modern Colchester.
2. Tacitus, *Annals* 14, 29–30.
3. Dio Cassius, *Roman History* 62, 1.
4. York.
5. Tacitus, *Agricola* 22–5.
6. Tacitus, *Agricola* 26.
7. Tacitus, *Agricola* 29–38. The battle actually took place in AD 84. The Romans were aware of Ireland, Hibernia, and, according to Tacitus, considered a full-scale invasion.

CHAPTER XII

OFF TO THE BATHS

Javolenus Priscus was glad to finish his day at the Basilica courts. Now he could relax, starting with a well-earned visit to the baths. So he got in his litter and headed for the nearest bath house where he would meet some friends, learn the latest news, and re-emerge a new man.

The baths and bathing were an essential facet of Roman life for men, women and children, rich and poor, slaves and free. Some very rich Romans had their own baths in their sumptuous houses, but most Romans availed themselves of the public baths. Baths were everywhere in Rome, as elsewhere – as ubiquitous as temples and bars and were said to number no less than 856 in Javolenus' day. Socialising in the baths was as routine as worshipping in those temples or drinking in those bars. Baths, with their conviviality and their often splendid architecture, were just good places to be; indeed, Javolenus Priscus could think of nowhere better to be as he paid his nominal entrance fee and entered the *thermae*. His particular favourite was the recently completed baths of Titus, next to Nero's Domus Aureus at the foot of the Esquiline Hill, opposite the Colosseum. What Javolenus really liked was the fact that the baths were a micro version of Rome itself with its shops, massage rooms, *palaestrae* or gymnasiums, and rest rooms, covered promenades; some top-end baths even boasted libraries, museums, and gardens.

But there were disadvantages, particularly if, like Seneca the Younger, you had the misfortune to live in a flat above a public bath house; in this letter to Lucilius he reveals a fascinating glimpse into what went on in these places:

> Imagine what a din reverberates in my ears! I have lodgings right over a bathing establishment. So picture the assortment of sounds, which are so loud as to make me hate my very powers of hearing! When your strongman, for example, is exercising himself by wielding lead weights, when he is working hard, or else pretends to be working hard, I can hear him grunt, and whenever he exhales his imprisoned breath, I can hear him panting, wheezy and hissing. Or perhaps I notice some lazy fellow, content with a cheap rubdown, and hear the crack of the pummelling hand on his shoulder, varying in sound according to whether that hand is laid on a flat or hollow part of the body … Add to this the arrest of the odd drunk or pickpocket, the noise of the man who always likes to sing out loud in the bath, or the over-keen men who plunge into the swimming pool splashing loudly.

View of the Baths of Titus by Giovanni Battista Piranesi (1720–78), circa 1775. Los Angeles County Museum of Art Link.

Photochrom of the 'Circular Bath' at the Roman Baths in Bath between 1890 and 1905. Library of Congress, Prints and Photographs Division, Photochrom Prints Collection.

Besides all of these ... picture the hair-plucker with his penetrating, shrill voice which he uses for self-advertising, – continually giving it vent and never shutting up except when he is plucking armpits and making his victim scream instead. Then the cake seller with his various cries, the sausage man, the sweet seller, and all the vendors of food hawking their wares, each with his own individual yell.

Seneca the Younger, *Letters* 56, 1, 2

Theft was a major problem too. Javolenus recalled how, when he was serving in Britannia, he would go to the baths at Aquae Sulis where a number of curse tablets were displayed excoriating thieves who stole bathers' possessions.[1] These were 'prayers for justice', for thefts of and restitution for thefts of jewellery, gemstones, money, household goods, and clothing. The inscriptions declared that the stolen property was transferred to a deity (Sulis) so that the loss is actually the deity's loss; the suspect is named and, often, the victim. The victim then invites the deity to visit afflictions on the thief, including death – not as a punishment, but to induce the thief to return the stolen items. One Javolenus particularly remembers went:

Solinus, to the goddess Sulis Minerva. I give to your divinity and majesty [my] bathing costume and cloak. Do not allow sleep or health to him who has done me wrong, whether man or woman or whether slave or free unless he reveals himself and brings those goods to your temple.

And another, cursing the thief with insanity and blindness:

Docimedis has lost two gloves and asks that the thief responsible should lose their minds and eyes in the goddess' temple.

Another names the suspects:

I have given to the goddess Sulis the six silver coins which I have lost. It is for the goddess to exact [them] from the names written below: Senicianus and Saturninus and Anniola.

To be on the safe side, Javolenus tipped the clothing attendant anyway.

The procedure in the baths was very logical: Javolenus dropped his clothes off at the *apodyterium,* or changing room, and went straight into the *sudatoria* to work up a sweat, and then the *frigidarium* (the cold water bath or swimming pool). He then progressed to the *tepidarium,* or warm room, followed by the *caldarium,* or a hot-water bath, sauna or steam room, with its underfloor heating courtesy of a brazier burning beneath the hollow floor. He then went back to the *tepidarium* to enjoy a massage with oils scraped off with a *strigil.*[2]

A whole army of beauty specialists were on hand to pander to his needs: Martial notes the *tractatrix* – the masseuse who spreads her practiced (*manus docta*) hand over every limb – the *unctores* (perfumers), *fricatores* (rubbers), *alipilarii* (depilators), and the *picatrices* (the girls who trimmed your pubic hair). The slaves then rubbed him down with towels made from the softest wool and wrapped him in a scarlet woollen cloak.

Then it was to the *laconium* – a dry, rest room to relax. Rest over, Javolenus went out into the *palaestra*, an open-air garden where he did some light exercise. Returning inside he bought a snack and some perfume and laid down to enjoy the marble mosaics on the floors, the stuccoed walls and their pastoral frescoes, the gold stars and celestial imagery up in the domes, and the statuary and fountains.

The frescoes here were by the famous artist Famulus whom Nero had commissioned to paint the celebrated Domus Aurea frescoes. Famulus specialised in large-scale mythological scenes; he favoured deep blue, green, indigo, purple, and cinnabar red. His works were dynamic and animated.

Mixed bathing was increasingly the norm in Javolenus' day, but in the Republic men and women bathers had been segregated. This inscription gives an illustration of how important mixed bathing was to a Roman:

> Pompeius urges passers-by to go and bathe in the baths of Apollo when they have finished reading the tombstone he has erected – he only wishes he could with his late wife, just like they used to.[3]

The *palaestra* was also important to Romans; it was where they could take exercise. Javolenus sometimes went there first for a workout before bathing. It was essentially a rectangular court surrounded by colonnades with rooms leading off for bathing, playing ball, just watching, or for storage of oil, dust for the hands, and athletic equipment. Here too was where the wrestlers wrestled – men and women, although not together.

We have Martial's obsequious Menogenes to thank for a description of the type of ball games played there, in a poem bewailing his persistent clamouring for an invitation to dinner:

> You can't escape Menogenes at the baths, hot or cold, although you try every which way to do so. He will catch your warm ball with his eager hands … he will pick up the football … from the dirt, and bring it you, even though he may have just got out of the bath and have his slippers on. If you bring linen with you, he will say it's whiter than snow, even though it's muckier than a baby's bib. If you comb what's left of your hair with the toothed ivory, he will say that you have a hair-do like Achilles. He will himself bring you the fetid dregs of the smoky wine jar, and will even wipe the sweat from your brow. He will praise everything, admire everything about you, until, after having patiently endured a thousand tortures, you utter the invitation, "Come dine with me!"
>
> Martial 12, 82

Notes

1. The 130 or so curse tablets found at Aquae Sulis (modern Bath) were from the second to the fourth centuries AD; however, there is nothing to suggest that similar curse tablets were not issued by angry bathers before that date and in the time Javolenus was in Britannia.
2. Pliny the Elder, *Natural History* 28, 55; Petronius, *Satyricon* 28; Martial 5, 42.
3. CIL 13, 2182.

Chapter XIII

Blood And Circuses

Today was a very special day for us in Rome.[1] Today, the emperor Titus attended the grand opening of the Flavian Amphitheatre in the city centre; it took ten years to build and was started by Titus' father, the emperor Vespasian, way back in AD 72.[2] Octavia and Julius were taken there by their mother and two slaves. This is what Octavia said about it:

Today is the first of 100 days of games: we joined the other 50,000 or so excited spectators but had to sit separately: we women and children were crammed in at the top at the back along with slaves and foreigners while the men had the better seats nearer the front: the more important the man, the nearer the front he sat. At least we are shaded from the sun while the men at the front bake in the sun. The six Vestal Virgins are the only women allowed in the front seats.

Nevertheless, there's free food and free entry for us; I suppose this is what Juvenal meant about bread and circuses?[3] It's the usual exciting programme: animal hunts (or man hunts depending on how you look at it), executions of criminals, then gladiator fights.

This huge audience comes from the four corners of the Empire: Sarmatians[4] who drink the blood of horses, Sygambrians[5] with their hair tied in a bun, faraway Britons and Arabs, Ethiopians with their dreadlocks. They say that 9,000 wild animals have been captured and shipped to Rome to appear in the games – most of them I've never seen before, except on wall paintings or mosaics.

What did I see? A mime about a robber crucified and torn to shreds by a Scottish bear; a slave playing Daedalus ripped apart by a bear; a re-enactment of the myth of Pasiphae and the bull; a raging rhinoceros charging a red ball as if it were a bull; a treacherous lion who bit his master and a bleeding bear speared by the hunters just like that pregnant pig whose piglet was born and scampered around its dying mother. The Daedalus act reminds me of the story about an Icarus who tried to fly at one of Nero's games; he fell out of the sky, close to the imperial couch and spattered the emperor with his blood.[6]

What else? An elephant actually kneels before Titus, a tigress bites a ferocious lion with its rabid fangs; the elephant gores a bull; a bull is lifted right up into the sky by some contraption from beneath the arena. The trainers aggravate a rhinoceros, anxious because it was taking so long for the mighty beast to get angry. The rhino eventually tossed a heavy bear with his twin horns just like a bull which throws stuffed dummies into the air. The rhino, its neck swivelling, hurls a pair of cows, overcomes a fierce oxen and a bison; a lion flees from him and runs straight onto the spears.

Two gladiators, Myrinus and Triumphus, do battle, but it's declared a draw, as is the duel between Verus and Priscus. And then a naval battle with ships in the flooded arena – unbelievable! Nereids, Neptune's tridents, oars, billowing sails on boats – they are all there – the sea battle to end all sea battles!

And it's not just men fighting – there's women down there too doing battle, not with the beasts but with dwarfs.[7] Some years ago, women gladiators shared their stage with an elephant walking on a tightrope – at games arranged by Nero in honour of his mother, Agripinna the Younger, whom he had recently murdered. The rather prim historian Tacitus was outraged at the sight of posh ladies of distinction and senators, disgracing themselves by performing in the amphitheatre.[8]

Not everyone, then, likes the games. Some people are repelled by them – Lucius Annaeus Seneca, the Stoic philosopher, being one. He said in a letter how he attended the games hoping for some wit and humour but was bitterly disappointed.[9] To him it was just sheer butchery. In the morning show, men were thrown to lions and to bears, but at midday they were thrown to the audience with no escape. The slayer was kept fighting until he was slain. 'Kill him! Flog him! Burn him alive', they yelled, 'Why is he such a coward?

The AD 80 Flavian amphitheatre, or Colosseum, in 2016.

Why won't he rush onto the swords? Why does he fall like a weakling? Why isn't he happy to die?' Seneca begs his friend, Lucilius, to stay away from the games because he will either be corrupted by the masses, or, if he shows his disgust, hated by them.

Bringing so many animals to Rome from far-flung areas of the empire was not without its problems. Pliny the Younger, in a letter to Valerius Maximus, laments the absence of some African panthers on the day of the games, delayed by a storm.[10]

Octavia goes on:

> Gladiators are our heroes, and great role models. They may be slaves but they have magical qualities: they say that their blood is used as a remedy for impotence and as an aphrodisiac; at their weddings, brides have her hair parted by a spear to ensure a fertile married life – ideally a spear which has been dipped in the blood of a defeated and dead gladiator. Doctors swear that drinking a gladiator's blood or eating his liver cures epileptics. Some gladiators have become 'A list' celebrities and are pictured in mosaics and sculptures, on lamps and tombstones; graffiti is scrawled about them; us girls love them and so do the boys, if they would admit to it.

Juvenal despises them though, but Martial wrote that they were a goldmine for the ticket touts. This what Juvenal had to say:

> How shameful is the woman who wears a helmet, who shuns femininity and loves brute force ... If a sale is held of your wife's effects, how proud you will be of her belt and arm-pads and plumes, and her half-length left-leg shin-guard! Hear her grunt while she practises thrusts from the trainer, wilting under the weight of the helmet.[11]

Octavia again:

> The other entertainment we enjoy is a day at the races. We go as a family to the Circus Maximus – the top venue for chariot racing with its huge 150,000 capacity.
>
> The races here are the last word in excitement: the racers are in teams – white and blue, green and red, servants hold the reins and excite the horses with encouraging pats to bring them up to a rapturous frenzy. Behind the barriers the beasts chafe – a steamy blast escapes from the wooden bars and the field is filled with their panting breath. They push, they bustle, they jostle, they struggle, they rage, they jump, they are frightened and they frighten; they kick the timbers. At last the herald with loud blaring trumpet calls the impatient teams to order and launches the swift chariots into the field.
>
> The ground gives way under the wheels and the air is clouded with dust as the drivers lash out, striking the horses' flanks while the sweat of drivers and flying steeds wets the field. They go round once, then a second time, then again; at the sixth lap the crowd is clamouring for a winner, but the leader is overtaken and the enemy goes for his wheel with a sideways dash. His horses are brought down, a multitude of legs tangle in the wheels, and the twelve spokes are shattered; another victim is flung from his chariot which falls on him in a heaving heap of havoc, and blood stains his forehead.[12]

Marble relief from Halicarnassus (first or second century AD) showing two female gladiators fighting; the inscription tells us that their names were Amazon and Achillia. Now in the British Museum (GR 1847. 4.24. 19).

Just watching with 150,000 people was nearly as exciting as actually racing. Not everyone is impressed, though; we know from our tutor that the younger Pliny just could not see the point of it – as he says in his letter to Calvisius. This was written when he was in Rome during the time of the Circensian games, an event which he found tasteless nothing new about them, same old boring stuff, nothing you'd want to see twice.[13] Pliny cannot see how so many thousands of people could be so like children, passionate about seeing time and time again a bunch of horses galloping round, and men standing up in their chariots. He could understand it if it were the speed of the horses, or the skill of the men that we the crowds loved. But it's not: it's the colours of the factions that we adore, and understanding that is beyond him.

When we're not at the games or the races, we might all go to the Campus Martius for a stroll and a game of something. In our geography lessons we read Strabo, and he is amazed by the size of the Campus because it can easily accommodate, not just the chariot-races and all other horse sports but also the crowds who play ball games and hoop rolling, and do wrestling.[14] There are some wonderful temples here and every year we celebrate the Anna Perenna during the Ides of March with the rest of Rome. This is a massive outdoor party with a day of feasting and drinking with much revelry. Tents are pitched or bowers are built from branches, boys meet girls, and people ask that Anna grant them as many more years as they can drink cups of wine at the festival.[15]

The Games are over now, the new amphitheatre is open, and we're on our way home.

Some years later, Octavia was able to attend the games given by Domitian (r. AD 81–96) for the Saturnalia with its magnificent festive extravaganza, as described by Statius (*Silvae* 1, 6):

The Calends of December

It was barely dawn when fruit and nuts rained down from the ropes[16] – the prevailing south easterly was spreading the dew: noble fruit from Pontic nut groves

A *retiarius* (left) and *secutor* (right) do battle. The former's weapons consisted of a barbed trident and weighted net.

or dates from the fertile fields of Idume[17], or the plums which pious Damascus grows on its branches, figs which bibulous Caunus ripens, all fall freely like great big booty. Biscuits and soft pastries; apples and pears from Ameria – masses of them, their ripeness just right, and laurel cake and bursting nut-shaped dates – all fell down from palm trees you couldn't see...

Look, more people are coming through the benches – a marvellous sight – they're all very well turned out and are as many as the people already sitting down in there. Some carry bread baskets and white napkins and even more sumptuous fare; others lavish languishing wine, you'd think they were as many as the servants of Ida! You are feeding, blessed Emperor, so many people; the circle of the great and good and, at the same time, the people who wear the toga – so let proud Annona [18] not know about this day. Come now Ancient of Days and compare our age more with the Golden Age of antique Jove: the wine didn't flow as freely then and the harvest didn't last the lazy year. One table feeds every rank: children, women, the common people, knights, senators: liberty has relaxed the usual reverence. Indeed, even you Emperor (what god could have so much time or promise as much you) even you come and share our banquet with us. Now Everyman, needy and fortunate alike, glories in the fact that he is the guest of the Emperor. Amid such clamour and unaccustomed luxuries the pleasure of the spectacle flew by. Women who have no experience in and who knew nothing about sword-craft got up and without embarrassment took on men's battles. You'd think that this was Thermodon's troops seething at Tanais or savage Phasis.[19] A brave company of dwarfs comes on: nature finished off creating them too soon and left them short and all bound up in a knotty lump. They take and dish out wounds in close combat and threaten to kill – what hands they have! Father Mars and bloody Bravery have a laugh at this and cranes waiting to fall on scattered booty are amazed by such ferocious fighters.

Now night's shadows draw in. What a tumult accompanies this distribution of largesse! Cheap girls come in now; you can see everything and anything fine and impressively skilful which the theatre audiences like. Here a crowd of big breasted Lydian girls clap their hands, there the tinkling symbols of Gades, there columns of Syrian soldiers raise a din, ordinary theatre goers and those who exchange common sulphur for powdered glass.[20]

In amongst all of this great flocks of birds all of a sudden swoop down from the sky: birds from the sacred Nile[21] and freezing Phasis[22], birds which the Numidians pick off in the dripping south. There aren't enough people to grab them all but they rejoice in filling the folds of their togas with their new booty. Voices, too many to count, are raised to the stars singing the praises of the Emperor's Saturnalia and they come to acclaim their Dominus with devoted affection. It had just got dark when a fireball fell glowing into the middle of the arena through the dark shadows brighter even than the starlight of the Gnosian coronet. The heavens were lit up like fire driving away the darkness of the night. Seeing this, lazy Quiet fled, and inert Sleep left for other cities. Who can sing of this spectacle, the endless fun, the partying, the free food, the floods of wine? Now that I am wasted by you Baccus, I drag myself drunk to sleep at last.

How many years from now will this day be remembered for? This holy day will never die out. For as long as the hills of Latium and old father Tiber remain, while your Rome still stands with the Capitol you have given back to the world, it will endure.

Notes

1. The date was AD 80.
2. Better known to us as the Colosseum; the name comes from the Colossus of Nero statue which stood nearby, itself named after the Colossus of Rhodes – one of the Seven Wonders of the World.
3. Juvenal was a contemporary satirical poet, born around AD 55. The 'bread and circuses' quotation is at Book 10, line 81. It means keeping the masses down by filling their bellies and providing some fun all free of charge.
4. From around the Danube.
5. A German tribe.
6. Later told by Suetonius (*c.* 69 – AD 122) at *Nero* 12, 1–2
7. Largely based on *On the Spectacles* by Martial. Nereids were sea nymphs. Martial (around AD 38 – AD 104) was a poet who came from Spain.
8. Tacitus, *Annals*, 15, 32. Tacitus: *c.* AD 56 – *c.* AD 120.
9. Lucius Annaeus Seneca (4 BC – AD 65); in *Epistles* 7, 3–5.
10. Pliny the Younger (61 AD – *c.* 113 AD); *Letters* 6,34.
11. Juvenal 6, 252ff; 82–103. A second-century AD marble relief from Halicarnassus (modern Bodrum) in Turkey (now in the British Museum) shows two women, Amazon and Achillia, fighting as gladiators. They are heavily armed like a secutor (a chaser of the retiarius, net man) with greaves and the right arm protected and carrying a large oblong shield; their hair is cropped in the style of a slave and their breasts are bare. Such a spectacle must have been important for it to be commemorated in this way. In September 2000, the Museum of London announced that they had discovered the grave of a female gladiator, from the first century AD – the first ever to be found. A piece of red pottery has been discovered with the inscription 'VERECVNDA LVDIA LVCIUS GLADIATOR', 'Verecunda the woman gladiator, Lucius the gladiator'.
12. Based on a description by Sidonius Apollinaris – *Poems* 23, 323-424, written in the fifth century AD.
13. Pliny the Younger, *Letters* 9, 6.
14. Strabo (64 BC – *c.* AD 24), *Geography* 5, 3, 8.
15. Ovid, *Fasti* 3, 523f. Anna Perenna was an ancient Roman goddess of the circle or 'ring' of the year, as the name (per annum) suggests. Macrobius, *Saturnalia* 1, 12, 6, records that offerings were made to her so that 'the circle of the year may be completed happily' and that people sacrificed to her both in public and in private.
16. Ropes were slung across the amphitheatre and from these the various delicacies were showered down on the crowds.
17. Modern Israel.
18. I.e. it's all free.
19. Amazons.
20. Rag and bone men.
21. Flamingos.
22. Pheasants.

CHAPTER XIV

COME DINE WITH ME

The family all came together for the evening meal, prepared and cooked by the slaves. Most Romans, the Priscus family included, usually ate simply at home, rejecting the tasteless pretentiousness and vulgar extravagance that came to characterise the middle-class dinner party. Three meals a day – breakfast, lunch, and dinner – was usual, with the latter, as here, being the main meal (the *cena*) taken early evening in the eighth or ninth hour.

Wheat-based food was the staple for the poorer people; the price of grain was kept artificially low after the legislation of Gaius Gracchus in 122 BC; the grain dole – free grain – was available to those who qualified after the law of Publius Clodius in 58 BC. This grain might be crushed and boiled into a type of porridge or into a *puls*, a couscous. The Romans probably also made pasta noodles – all as main courses, rather than side dishes. Where a family could afford an oven, then the grain might be made into bread. Other popular foods were beans, leeks, and sheep's lips; depending on your wealth, a selection of meats, *garum* (a fish sauce); cheeses, fruits, and vegetables were also an option. Wine was the drink of choice: the better off you were, the better the wine, with something approximating vinegar for the poorest people; whatever the quality, wine was usually mixed with water.

The Priscus family dined in their *triclinium* – Javolenus and Caecilia reclining on their couch with the children seated on stools in front of them.

Fish sauce made from the blood and intestines of fish (*garum* or *liquamen*) was a very popular staple. *Garum* factories sprang up in towns near to the sea and have been excavated at Barcino, Barcelona, and at Pompeii. A recipe can be found in the *Geoponica* (20, 46, 1–5), a twenty-book collection of agricultural lore and animal husbandry, compiled during the tenth century in Constantinople for the Byzantine emperor Constantine VII Porphyrogenitus. *Garum* from Lusitania was particularly prized.

Caecilia never tires of telling Ovid's didactic story of Philemon and Baucis, rich in family values and a lesson in frugality – and good for Octavia and Julius to hear, however often. It describes a typical peasant meal, in which Jupiter and Mercury are conducting some door-to-door research to gauge the hospitality of the people of Phrygia in Asia Minor. A thousand doors were slammed in their faces when they knocked and asked for food and shelter; however, when they reached the humble abode of long-married and loyal Philemon and Baucis, they were served a meal, which, though frugal, was sumptuous even by their own divine standards. The gods eventually revealed their true identities and granted the couple a wish: Philemon and Baucis wished that they would die together so that neither one of them would ever have to live alone. Jupiter and Mercury obliged by changing them into trees when their time had come. The story not only emphasises the virtues of humility, parsimony, and hospitality, but it also celebrates marital harmony, lasting love and affection – so often diminished in the venal and permissive times of Titus' reign and deplored by Caecilia.

> [Baucis] stripped some cabbage leaves, which her good husband had picked for the meal. Then with a two-pronged fork Philemon fetched down from a beam a side of smoked bacon, and cut a small portion from the shank which had been smoked for ages. He tenderised it in boiling water … And over here are green and black olives, fruit of chaste Minerva, and the cornel berries, autumn-picked and pickled – these were served for relish; and endive, and radishes surrounding a large pot of cheese; and eggs not overdone but gently turned in glowing embers – all served up on earthenware dishes. Then sweet wine served in clay jugs, so expensive – all embossed! … Next they served up new wine, mellow this time; and a second course: sweet nuts, dried figs and wrinkled dates and plums, and scented apples, heaped up in wide baskets; and – almost hidden in a wreath of grapes from purple vines – a glistening honey-comb. All these orchard treats were enhanced by a desire by Baucis and Philemon to please [their guests]. With happy smiles … this aged couple, anxious to share their most valued possession, began to chase after the only goose they had – the faithful guardian of their little home – which they would kill and offer to the Gods. But swift of wing, it eventually wore them out, and took refuge with those smiling Gods.
>
> Ovid, *Metamorphoses* 8, 646–678

By contrast, the dinner party could be a vulgar and prodigal affair. Horace describes the hideous and toe-curling pretentiousness often displayed on such occasions: add to this the extravagance, gluttony, waste, one-upmanship, indulgent exoticism of the menu, bizarre entertainments, boring and boorish hosts, and we are left with a thoroughly dismal dining experience.

Petronius' *Cena Trimalchionis* provides the pinnacle, embracing all the horrors of a meal at the flashy, trashy home of a nouveau riche in small town Italy.

Martial shows us just how essential a diary full of dinner invitations was in the social lives of some people, and how disastrous a day it was if it ended with a solitary meal at home. At 12, 82 he describes the lengths some people go to secure an invitation. The vulgar behaviour of some diners is described in the other poems: his doggy-bag guest is anticipated by Catullus' napkin thief (Carmen 112) and echoes his description of the gluttony of a guest in 7, 20. To Horace and Pliny, meanness, though, is just as reprehensible as greed and extravagance.

Elsewhere, Martial neatly sums up the excesses of one country house dinner party (3, 17) and, by contrast, describes his own menu, positively modest and restrained by a Trimalchio's standards (5, 78). Pliny reinforces the importance of protocol in *Letters* 1, 15 when he deplores the failure of an invited guest to show up. Martial's even-handedness

A family meal showing three generations of a Roman family. A first-century AD painting from Pompeii, now in the Museo Archeologico, Naples.

and fairness in insisting on serving the same food to all the guests, whatever their social status, is reflected in his attack on dinner time discrimination in 10, 49.

Here is what Horace had to say:

"How did you enjoy your dinner party with good old Nasidienus? When I was looking for you yesterday to be my guest they told me that you had been drinking there since midday."

"I had the time of my life."

"Tell me then, if it's not too much trouble, what was the first course to satisfy your grumbling stomach?"

"First up was a Lucanian boar ... dressed with bitter-tasting turnips, lettuces, radishes – the sort of stuff that revives a tired stomach – skirrett, fish sauce and Coan tartar...Next, like an Attic virgin bearing the sacred emblem of Ceres, dusky Hydaspes entered with Caecuban wine and then Alcon with Chian – and it hadn't been diluted with sea water. Our host asked: "Maecenas, if you'd prefer Alban or Falernian to this, we have both."

"Wealth is obnoxious! ... The rest of the mob, us I mean, ate fowl, oysters and fish; it all tasted very different from what we were used to; this very quickly became apparent when he offered us livers of turbot and plaice – something we had not tasted before. After this he informed me that the honey apples were red because they had been picked by the light of a waning moon – why that makes a difference you'd best ask him."

"Then Vibidius said to Balatro: "If we don't drink him out of house and home we will die unavenged' – and he called for bigger goblets. At this our host's face turns white: nothing did he fear more than hardened drinkers – either because they're only too ready to bad-mouth you or because full-bodied wines blunt a delicate palate. Vibidius and Balatro decanted full jugs of wine into Allifan goblets; everyone else followed suit except those guests on the bottom couch who did the flagons no damage at all.

"Then they brought in a lamprey sprawled on a platter with shrimps swimming around it. On this the master remarked: 'This lamprey was pregnant when it was caught; the flesh isn't so good after spawning. The sauce is mixed as follows: oil from Venafrum – the first pressing only – roe from the sauce of a Spanish mackerel, five year vintage Italian wine poured in while warm – warmed Chian is the best – white pepper and don't forget vinegar made from fermenting grapes from Lesbos. It was I who introduced bitter elecampane and greens boiled in the sauce. Curtillus uses unwashed sea urchins because the juices from the sea shells are better than just sea water ... Next the servants came in parading the carved up limbs of a crane on a huge platter, liberally seasoned with salt and lots of flour; the liver of a snow goose stuffed with juicy figs; and a hare with its legs ripped off – much nicer that way than with them still on. Then we saw blackbirds, their breasts roasted and rumpless doves served up to us: special stuff this – our host told us all about the why and wherefore of each of them. We got our revenge by running out without trying any of it, just as if Canidia the witch had breathed all over the food – and her breath's worse than an African snake's."

Horace, *Satires* 2, 8

Here are excerpts from Trimalchio's famous feast – a picaresque description of small town nouveau riche Italy, with episode after vulgar episode of extravagance, pretentiousness, and outrageous ostentation as sumptuous dinner courses are punctuated by bizarre entertainments:

We finally got to recline and some of the Alexandrian boys poured snow-cold water over our hands; others followed and at our feet skilfully gave us pedicures ... The hors d'oeuvres really whetted our appetites; everyone was reclining now except Trimalchio himself who was to be on the top table in the new fashion. A bronze baby saddle-back donkey stood on the tray, black olives on one side, white on the other. Two dishes hid the donkey, on the edge Trimalchio's name and their weight in silver were inscribed. There were even dormice seasoned with honey and pepper held up on little bridges that had been soldered on. Sizzling sausages had been placed on a silver grill and under the grill Syrian plums and Punic pomegranates…

We were still on the starters when a tray was brought in with a basket on it; in here was a wooden cockerel, its wings splayed out in a circle as they do when they are laying eggs. Two slaves came up now and, with the music at full blast, began to rummage through the straw; they plucked out pea-hen's eggs and shared them among the guests ... then a slave brought in a silver skeleton made in such a way that its joints and vertebrae could be articulated and bent in every direction. He threw it down onto the table once or twice so that the moving joints took on different poses ... As we applauded this another course followed – clearly not as big as we'd hoped but its sheer originality had everyone agog. The twelve zodiacal signs were arranged in a circle on a round tray; on each of the signs the chef had placed food fitting and appropriate to the sign. Over Aries ram-shaped chickpeas; over Taurus a piece of beef; over Gemini testicles and kidneys; over Cancer a garland; over Leo an African fig; over Virgo the womb of a virgin sow; over Libra a set of scales with a tart on one side and a cake on the other; over Scorpio little sea fish; over Sagittarius a lamprey; over Capricorn a lobster; over Aquarius a goose; over Pisces a pair of red mullets. In the middle a honeycomb lay on a grassy clump of turf. An Egyptian boy was going round with bread on a silver bread tray ... Trimalchio then proceeded to murder a song from the mime Laserpiciario, his voice hideous. It was with some reluctance that we approached our low rent meal. Trimalchio said "Come on let's dine – here's the menu." As he spoke four dancers came in to a fanfare and lifted off the top part of the dish. This enabled us to see fat fowls and sows' udders at the bottom and in the middle a hare was dressed up in wings to look like Pegasus. Around the corners of the dish we picked out four figures of Marysas; the dancers drizzled a peppery fish sauce from their wine bottles over some fish which were swimming in a channel...

"Bravo!" we all shouted together and with hands raised high swore that Hipparchus and Aratus were no match for him. The servants came in and placed valances over the couches; nets were painted on these and ambushers with hunting spears and all the paraphernalia of the hunt. We still didn't know what to expect next when a mighty roar came from outside the dining room and Spartan hounds began running round the tables. A platter was then brought in with the biggest wild boar on it you'd ever seen. It was wearing the felt cap of freedom, and two little baskets interwoven with dates hung from its tusks – one filled with nut-shaped dates, the other with Theban dates. Around it were little piglets made from cake looking as if they were about to suck the udders; this told us that we had before us a breeding sow. They were the gifts for the guests to take home with them. Carver, who had hacked up the fattened fowls, did not step forward to carve up the boar but instead a huge bearded bloke, his legs strapped with bands and wearing a woven hunting tunic, did the honours. He drew a hunting knife and slashed the flank of the boar hard with it. At this blow thrushes flew out from inside the boar.

Petronius, *Satyricon: Cena Trimalchionis*, 26–36; 39–41

Martial deplores a dinner guest's rude habit of stealing the meal:

You hoover up whatever is served up for you: the udders of a sow, the rib of a pork, a hazel hen for two to share, a half-eaten mullet and a whole sea bass, a side of murena, a chicken's leg, a wood pigeon dripping in its sauce. When you have concealed all this in your soggy napkin you give it to your boy to carry home. We recline – an idle lot. If you have any shame – bring back our meal Caecilianus: I didn't invite you here today so that you can feast tomorrow.

Martial 2, 37

The Apicius is the place to go for a peerless Roman recipe book; compiled in the late fourth or early fifth century AD, it is often referred to as the *De Re Coquinaria* of *Apicius*. Here are some tempting examples:

Brain Sausage (*Isicia de Cerebellis*)

Put in the mortar pepper, lovage and origany, moisten with broth and rub; add cooked brains and mix diligently so that there be no lumps. Incorporate five eggs and continue mixing well to have a good forcemeat which you may thin with broth. Spread this out in a metal pan, cook, and when cooked cold unmould it onto a clean table. Cut into a handy size. Now prepare a sauce. Put in the mortar pepper, lovage and origany, crush, mix with broth. Put into a sauce pan, boil, thicken and strain. Heat the pieces of brain pudding in this sauce thoroughly, dish them up, sprinkled with pepper, in a mushroom dish.

Flamingo and Parrot (*In phoenicoptero*)

Scald the flamingo, wash and dress it, put it in a pot, add water, salt, dill, and a little vinegar, to be parboiled. Finish cooking with a bunch of leeks and coriander, and add some reduced must to give it color. In the mortar crush pepper, cumin, coriander, laser root, mint, rue, moisten with vinegar, add dates, and the fond of the braised bird, thicken, strain, cover the bird with the sauce and serve. Parrot is prepared in the same manner.

Milk-fed Snails (*Cochleas lacte pastas*)

Take snails and sponge them; pull them out of the shells by the membrane and place them for a day in a vessel with milk and salt. Renew the milk daily. Hourly clean the snails of all refuse, and when they are so fat that they can no longer retire to their shells fry them in oil and serve them with wine sauce. In a similar way they may be fed on a milk porridge.

Stuffed Dormouse (*Glires*)

Stuff with a forcemeat of pork and small pieces of dormouse meat trimmings, all pounded with pepper, nuts, laser, broth. Put the dormouse thus stuffed in an earthen casserole, roast it in the oven, or boil it in the stock pot.

CHAPTER XV

PETS AND PLAY

As with many Roman children, Octavia and Julius have a pet dog, Cerberus; as with all Roman children, Octavia and Julius played games either with each other or with their friends.

One of the paradoxes in Roman society is how the Romans showed great affection towards their family pets but, at the same, time clamoured to watch other animals butchered by gladiators or ripping one another to bits in the arena. It seems that on one day Romans could grieve over and bury their deceased pets with fondness, and the very next day would go to the games and watch scores of lions, rhinos, and other such magnificent beasts massacred before their eyes, baying for their blood.

Perhaps the most famous family pet is the guard dog on the *cave canem* ('beware of the dog') mosaic from Pompeii; similar notices would have been displayed all over Rome and the Roman Empire. This, and Catullus' *passer*, sparrow (or bullfinch), poems (Carmen 2 and 3) and a number of epigraphs and other literary references to companion animals tell us that the family pet was alive and well in ancient Rome.

Not all pets were cute. The nice Priscus pet shared nothing with these brutes – kept more for reasons of security than mutual affection. That mosaic, from the entrance to the House of the Tragic Poet, warns us that a dangerous dog is on guard within, even though it is clearly chained up. Petronius describes a similar scene: 'There on the left as

Children playing various games with nuts, as depicted on a marble panel from a sarcophagus, third century AD. From Vigna Emendola on the Via Appia. Now in the Museo Chiaramonti, Rome.

you go in ... was a huge dog with a chain round its neck. It was painted on the wall and over it, in block capitals, was written: Beware of the Dog' (Petronius, *Satyricon* 29). Some archaeologists have, contrarily, argued that the warning was for visitors to be careful not to tread on the small dogs within, possibly Italian greyhounds.

Elsewhere, Molossian hounds are described as baying, terrifying guard dogs in Horace's tale of the town and country mice (*Satires* 2, 6), while we have seen Spartan hounds run amok in Trimalchio's dinner party (Petronius, *Satyricon* 40). Lucretius describes Molossian guard dogs in his *De Rerum Natura* (5, 1063–72), while Petronius introduces his huge, chained guard dog Scylax to his dinner guests as guardian of home and slaves (*Satyricon* 64). The beast reappears when Trimalchio's guests try to escape, its barking sending two of them headlong into the fish pool. Meanwhile, Croesus, Trimalchio's boyfriend, has foolishly encouraged his obese black pet puppy, Margarita, to attack Scylax – who responds by ripping the puppy almost to shreds.

A century or so before that dog was prowling around The House of the Tragic Poet, the love poet Catullus composed his poems, with distinct erotic undertones, celebrating his mistresses' pet sparrow (*passer*): Catullus' *passer* poems, and the keeping of birds as pets, were influential with poets over the next hundred or so years. Ovid wrote an elegy on the death of Corinna's parrot (*psittacus*):

> Parrot, the mimic, the winged one from India's East,
> is dead – Go, birds, form a flock and follow him to the grave!...
> A burial mound holds his bones – a burial mound that is just the right size –
> whose little stone carries a fitting epitaph for him:
> "His grave holds one who gave pleasure to his mistress:
> his speech to me was cleverer than the speech of other birds".
>
> Ovid, *Amores*, 2, 6, 1–2; 59–62

Indeed, Cerberus, despite his name, has much more in common with Publius' over-indulged and fawning Issa:

> Issa is naughtier than Catullus's sparrow. Issa is purer than the kiss of a dove. Issa is more loving than any young girl. Issa is dearer than Indian jewels. The little dog Issa is the pet of Publius. If she complains, you would think she was speaking. She feels both her master's sorrow and the joy. She lies reclined upon his neck, and sleeps, so that not a breath is heard from her ... So that her final hour may not carry her off completely, Publius has had her portrayed in a picture, in which you will see an Issa so life-like, that not even she is so like herself. In a word, place Issa and the picture side by side, and you will imagine either both real, or both painted.
>
> Martial 1, 109

We can add a number of other popular avian pet species to the *passer* and the *psittacus*: nightingales, starlings, ravens, and magpies, for example. Looking back over centuries of the pet 'talking' nightingales, Clement of Alexandria was forced to chastise those people who kept them as pets, along with parrots and curlews, rather than discharging their responsibility to look after their fellow humans. Indeed, Seneca the Younger was no less

Children playing ball games, detail. Marble, Roman artwork of the second quarter of the second century AD. Louvre Museum Department of Greek, Etruscan and Roman Antiquities. Photographer Marie-Lan Nguyen.

intolerant in Javolenus' time when he referred to those who 'thought nothing of raising puppies and birds and other silly pets'.[1]

Sentimentality and affection, however, were probably more typical of the average Roman's attitude to the household pet, as evidenced by Petronius when he tells of a father who kills his son's pet gold finches – his son who is 'mad on birds' – but it is, nevertheless, a silly hobby according to the father who lies that a weasel killed them.[2] Martial's menagerie of pets that his acquaintances indulge perhaps indicates their general popularity, and Martial's contempt for such people. We have a long-eared fox or lynx (*lagalopex*); a gazelle (*dorcas*); Publius's lapdog (as mentioned above); an ugly long-tailed monkey just as ugly as Comius, its owner; a mischievous Egyptian rat; a garrulous magpie; a neck-curling cold skinned serpent; and Telesilla's deceased nightingale, for which she was sufficiently bereaved to erect a burial mound. To Martial, they are all just monsters (*monstra*).[3]

By the early empire, spoiled pets were getting their own solemn funeral epithets, a practice which began with the Greeks in the Hellenistic age.[4] The popular green Indian parrot answered a desire for talking birds, and, according to Pliny the Elder, even greeted emperors; they were, he adds, particularly talkative after a sip of wine: *in vino psittacus*.[5] Pliny tells the story of the shoemaker who owned a raven, which was in the habit of greeting Tiberius, Germanicus, and Drusus Caesar; whether the bird ever succeeded in cheering up the notoriously gloomy Tiberius is not recorded, but we do know that on its death it was buried with great ceremony and many a floral tribute. The bier was carried by two Ethiopians preceded by a flautist along the Appian Way. A neighbouring cobbler had killed the bird out of angry jealousy, claiming that its droppings had splattered his shoes; he was lynched for his troubles by the even angrier mob. Pliny draws an amusing comparison when he acidly points out that no one ever avenged the death of Scipio Aemilianus – even after he had gone to the trouble of eliminating Carthage and Numantia for Rome.

The novelist Apuleius reveals that teaching a parrot to swear is pointless: it simply results in an endless repertoire of expletives; the only remedy then is to cut out its tongue or return it to the wild.[6] Pliny the Younger writes of the bonfire of family pets made by Regulus on the funeral pyre of his young son to ensure he enjoyed the pets in the afterlife:

> The boy had a few ponies, some in harness and others not broken in, dogs both big and small, nightingales, parrots and blackbirds – Regulus slew all of these at his pyre.
>
> Pliny, *Letters* 4, 2, 3

Excavations around Roman camps in Britannia have yielded up the bones of ravens – soldiers' pets, no doubt. Persius, Statius, Petronius, and Pliny all mention magpies that kept sentinel on thresholds to greet visitors.[7] We also hear that Nero's mother, Agrippina, owned a talking pet thrush – the first of its kind at Rome. Britannicus and Nero, as young boys, had a starling and nightingales that spoke Latin and Greek; the

'Cave canem!' Pompeii's 'beware of the dog' mosaic notice found in the House of the Tragic Poet.

Hellenistic mosaic of a dog with overturned bronze vessel found in 1993 during the excavations of the royal palaces at Alexandria.

birds practiced every day and added constantly to their vocabulary. 'Tuition' took place in a private room with a (human) teacher and nothing to disturb the intensive wrote learning ('parrot fashion'?) that was encouraged and motivated by titbits.[8] Sometimes parrots, some of which may have been originally kept as pets, ended up on the dinner plate, as suggested by Apicius' recipe.[9] We also hear of a saluting crow and a loquacious magpie.[10] Columella recommends keeping peacocks as pets because of their beauty. He is also a devotee of geese, which make excellent guards, better even than dogs; the legend of the cackling geese that famously alerted the Romans during the 390 BC attack by the Gauls is called to mind; the guard dogs disappointingly remaining silent.[11] Julius Caesar tells us that the Britons did not eat hare, goose or chicken, but did keep them for pleasure.[12] Pet hares feature in wall paintings: one from Trastevere depicts the endearing scene of a woman musician being presented with a baby hare; two paintings from Rome show hares on their haunches on the knees of girls, while a tombstone (now in Lincoln cathedral) has the scene of a boy cuddling his pet hare.

Cats too made popular pets. The first evidence of domestic cats in Italy comes from silver coins from the fifth century BC minted in Tarentum and Rhegium on which, for

Pergamon Museum, Berlin parrot mosaic. Early to mid-second century BC.

example, a boy plays with a cat, teasing it with either a bird or a morsel of food, or where the cat plays with a ball. Cats also star on Apulian and Campanian vases, examples of which are in the British Museum and depict cats either playing with balls or, in one case, confronting a goose. The most celebrated images of cats come, of course, from two mosaics found in Pompeii. One shows a cat pawing a partridge with two ducks and other potential meals; the other depicts a cat threatening two parrots and a dove perched precariously close on the rim of a bowl.

Diodorus Siculus tells us how a Roman soldier serving in Egypt in the reign of Ptolemy XI Alexander II (r. 80 BC) was attacked by an angry mob when he killed a cat by mistake (1, 71). Cats, of course, were treated as kings and gods in Egypt; Herodotus had famously written that if a cat died in the house then the occupants shaved off their eyebrows.[13] The Egyptian word for a cat was '*maou*' – the last word in onomatopoeia. Cicero, Ovid, Seneca, and Pliny all refer to house cats.[14]

The Romans enjoyed many other pets. Paintings on vases and reliefs show goats yoked to children's carts while a Pompeian wall painting depicts a woman feeding a branch to a goat in her bedroom. Cicadas competed with songbirds to provide musical entertainment; eleven epigrams describe these pets chirruping away in their specially made reed and osier cages.[15] Pliny, Plutarch, Aulus Gellius, Appian, and Frontinus all refer to Sertorius' pet white fawn.[16] A Dresden terracotta shows a boy with a bowl and a mouse sitting on the rim.

Evidence for pet monkeys go back to the third century BC and Plautus when he refers to one in the *Miles Gloriousus*: old Periplectomonos from Ephesus commands his slaves to remove anyone found on his roof pretending to be up there to catch the monkey (160–163); in the *Mercato*, Demipho describes a dream in which he gives a nanny goat to a tame monkey to look after (229–233). A Cathaginian boy is bitten on the hand

A menagerie of animals in this mosaic in the Pergamon Museum, Berlin.

by his pet monkey in the *Poenulus* (1,073). Pliny describes the pride shown by tame monkeys for their young, which were born in the house, showing them off, encouraging people to stroke them and hugging them; indeed sometimes hugging them too tightly and cuddling them to death.[17]

Tame, trained, and bejewelled fish were all the rage. Cicero sneers at the people who think they have died and gone to heaven when the bearded mullet they keep in their ponds feed from their hands.[18] Martial delights in the myriad fish at balmy Formiae, which swim obediently towards their master who is enjoying some leisurely, effortless fishing.[19] Pliny tells how Antonia Minor adorned her lamprey with gold and earrings and how they were passed down to Claudius and then to Agrippina, mother of Nero, after Antonia's death as an heirloom.[20]

When not playing with Cerberus, Julius and Octavia had a range of games they would play. One of the most exciting was *harpastum* – a small ball contact game, which was played at considerable speed and required agility and energy. Martial refers to it when describing Atticus' preference for running:

No hand-ball (*pila*), no bladder-ball (*follis*), no feather-stuffed ball (*paganica*) makes you ready for the warm bath, nor the blunted sword-stroke upon the unarmed stump; nor do you stretch forth squared arms besmeared with oil, nor, darting to and fro, snatch the dusty ball (*harpasta*), but you just run by the clear Virgin water (the Aqua Virgo aqueduct).

Martial 7, 32

In *follis* (balloon-ball) the idea was to prevent a leather ball from touching the ground by batting it back with the fist or forearm.

Trigon was played with three players standing at the corners of a triangle with a hard ball that does not bounce. The object was to throw the ball to another player in the hope that he or she could not catch it. Feinting played a part in this game and two balls could be in play at the same time. Skill was demonstrated by catching a ball left-handed, as was transferring the ball from one hand to the other. Batting a ball back rather than catching it was also a sign of skill. Missing a catch and being hit by the ball was a score for the opponent.

When they tired of the ball games, the children could always resort to rolling the hoop (*trochus*).

Notes

1. Seneca, *Ad Marciam* 12, 2.
2. Petronius, *Satyricon* 46, 5.
3. Martial 7, 87.
4. See, for example, *IG* 14, 56 (Sicilia) and *CIG* 3559.
5. Pliny, *NH* 10, 42; 10, 121–2.
6. Apuleius, *Florida* 12.
7. Persius *Prologus* 8–14; Pliny *NH* 10, 42, 118–9; Petronius, *op. cit.* 28, 9; Statius, *Silvae* 2, 4, 19.
8. Pliny, op. cit. 10, 120.
9. *Apicius* 5, 6, 1.
10. Martial 3, 95; 14, 74; 14, 76.
11. *De Re Rustica* 8, 11.
12. *De Bello Gallico* 5, 12.
13. Herodotus 2, 66.
14. Ovid, *Metamorphoses* 5, 33; Seneca, *Epistles* 121; Pliny, *op. cit.* 10, 73; 11, 37. Palladius (fl. AD 350) is the first to use the word *cattus* in his Opus *Agriculturae* (20, 8) when he bizarrely recommends them for catching moles in artichoke beds. On a larger scale, Evagrius (*c.* AD 593) tells us that, as a boy, St Simeon Stylites walked his tame pet panther around on a lead (*Historia Ecclesiastica* 6, 23). In two of his epigrams, Agathias (AD 527–565) records that his house-born cat ate his tame partridge when it should have been pursuing mice (*Anthologia Palatina* 7, 204; 7, 205). Aetius recommended inserting the liver of a cat inside a tube fitted to the woman's left foot as a contraceptive device. We get some interesting images of domesticated cats in Roman sculpture. There is a fine example of one on a sarcophagus from the first half of the first century AD inscribed with the occupant's name, Calpurnia Felicla – 'pussy' (CIL 6, 14223). In the Capitoline Museum in Rome, we can see a cat being trained to dance by a woman to the strains of a lyre with a tempting brace of birds suspended above it. The Musée des Antiques in

8

Bordeaux has on display a delightful relief showing a girl holding a kitten while a cockerel pecks at its tail. In Auxerre Museum, a fragmentary statuette has a cat wearing a collar.

15. AP 7, 189; 190, 192–8, 200, 201.
16. Pliny, *op. cit.* 3, 82; Plutarch, *Sertorius* 11; Aulus Gellius 15, 32; Appian, *Bellum Civile* 1, 13, 110; Frontinus, *Strategematon* 1, 11, 13.
17. Pliny, *op. cit.* 8, 80.
18. *Ad Atticum* 2, 1, 7.
19. 10, 30, 22–4.
20. *Op. cit.* 9, 55. Varro tells us about his friend, Quintus Hortensius, the orator, who would rather sell a mule than a bearded mullet. Hortensius was just as concerned when his fish were sickening as he was over an ill slave. When his *murena* died, he wept. When Julius Caesar was celebrating a triumph and wanted Gaius Hirrius's *murenae* to show off at his banquets, Gaius Hirrius refused to sell them and would only lend them to Caesar: Varro (3, 17, 3) puts the number of fish at 2,000, Pliny at 6,000 (NH 9, 81). According to Martial (4, 30, 3–7), Domitian had a fish pool at Baiae populated with fish that had been given personal names, recognised the emperor and came swimming up to lick his hand when he called their names.

Mosaics from Pompeii showing a cat with bird (above), and ducks and fish (below).

CHAPTER XVI
AND SO TO BED

At the end of a busy day the Priscus family, and their slaves, retired to their various bedrooms and beds.

How much sleep they manage to get depends entirely on how much noise disturbs them from the streets outside. Octavia would sleep well – that is if she was not plagued by the notorious bogeywomen. These diluted versions of witches were insinuated into the impressionable minds of children in cautionary tales. The bogeywoman often appeared as a big bad wolf that ate naughty boys and girls alive and always had one freshly devoured in her stomach.

The ubiquitous bogeywoman took the shape of Mormo; she was either queen of the Lystraegones, who had lost her own children and now murdered others, or a child-eating Corninthian. Another was Empusa, who variously took the form of a cow, donkey, or beautiful woman, and yet another was Gello, an evil female spirit and child snatcher. To Diodorus Siculus, Empusa was a beautiful child-eater. The Romans also had Lamia – a vivacious Libyan woman whose children by Zeus were murdered by Hera; like Mormo she was a cannibal and exacted revenge by murdering other women's babies, eating them alive.

A scene likely to scare young children at bedtime? Two women consulting a witch with all three wearing theatre masks. Roman mosaic from the Villa del Cicerone in Pompeii, now in the Museo Archeologico Nazionale, Naples. By Dioscorides of Samos.